NorthLink
FERRIES

Passage to the Northern Isles
Ferry Services to Orkney & Shetland 1790-2010

MILES COWSILL *and* COLIN SMITH

Published by: Ferry Publications, PO Box 33, Ramsey, Isle of Man IM99 4LP
Tel: +44 (0) 1624 898445   Fax: +44 (0) 1624 898449   E-mail: FerryPubs@manx.net   Website: www.ferrypubs.co.uk

Introduction

In 1999 Ferry Publications published 'The North Boats', the work of the late Alastair McRobb, which offered a full account of the ferry and passenger shipping operations to the Orkney and Shetland islands, for which he had a great passion and followed for many years. Alastair had the advantage of a career at sea serving in ships of the North of Scotland, Orkney and Shetland Shipping Company Ltd – the North Company which motivated him to follow the marine operations of the company in great detail for over 50 years. The publication proved to be an overwhelming success, selling not only in Shetland and Orkney but also worldwide as there has always been great interest in the historical and fascinating ships that have served these islands.

In 2002 NorthLink took over the ferry routes to the islands from P&O Scottish Ferries. A major shift and modernisation in the operations was to take place with the introduction of three new purpose-built ships to serve Orkney and Shetland. NorthLink not only offered an enhanced style and standard of service but the introduction of their new ferries has opened new markets and has generated substantial growth of tourist traffic to the islands.

Those who travel on the services to the islands as 'locals', will know that the shipping operations play a vital role in their everyday life for provisions and trade. The island lifeline operated by NorthLink has to be maintained 52 weeks of the year and the current fleet has proved to be very reliable in this role. For those who travel as visitors to Orkney and Shetland, it is a fascinating journey to two distinctive island groups, which are fiercely independent in their own way from each other and from mainland Scotland with each island in each group offering its own charm and individual experience.

In this new edition we bring the history of the 'North Boats' up to date to 2010. This book includes many pictures of the former "North Company" ships that have never previously been published and many others which span all periods of the shipping operations from P&O to the present day. We hope that they add to the updated and revised text to provide a fascinating publication for everyone who has a passion for the Northern Isles and for the ships that have served them today and in the past.

We would like to thank Bill Davidson, Managing Director, NorthLink for all his help and encouragement with this book. The following should also be thanked for going that extra mile for us with photos and information for the title: Bruce Peter, Andrew MacLeod, Lawrence MacDuff, John Manson, David Parsons, Willie Mackay, Elaine Tulloch, Magnus Dixon, STX Europe and all the staff at NorthLink.

Colin Smith, Glamis, Scotland &
Miles Cowsill, Isle of Man

March 2010

*Showing the style and looks of a private yacht, the **St. Sunniva** (II) was probably one of the most beautiful vessels to serve the Northern Isles. (Bruce Peter collection)*

*The **St Clair II** laid up at Aberdeen nearing the end of her 30 year career.*
(Bruce Peter collection)

Foreword

It gives me great pleasure to have been able to contribute to the production of this latest edition of the definitive book documenting the history of the "North Boats" from the days of sail to the current era of NorthLink Ferries. When it comes to recording European ferry history, the publishers, Ferry Publications, are the acknowledged masters.

Bill Davidson

NorthLink has been operating on the routes for a little over seven years and, as such, we are relative newcomers to the Orkney and Shetland shipping scene. Nevertheless, I am acutely aware that, following in the wakes of our illustrious predecessors, we have inherited the mantle of lifeline service operators and that we should strive, always, to be upholders of the highest standards for seamanship and passenger service.

From the days of the original North Company, through to our predecessors P&O Scottish Ferries, and into the twenty first century, the North Boats have always been at the heart of the island communities we serve and it gives all at NorthLink a great sense of pride to know that we carry on those finest traditions in the modern ships of today.

I am sure that everyone who has an interest in Orkney, Shetland and the history of the shipping routes to the islands will find something of interest in this book. From NorthLink's perspective, I am very aware of the proud heritage of which our company is now part and I know that all of our officers, crews, shore staff and the many contractors in the wider NorthLink family continue to take great pride in our fleet, our services and the communities which they and their predecessors have served for almost two centuries.

Bill Davidson
Chief Executive
NorthLink Ferries Ltd
March, 2010

*The reception area on the **Hjaltland**. (Miles Cowsill)*

*The **St. Clair** (III) at Victoria Pier, Lerwick. (David Parsons)*

From Sail to P&O Scottish Ferries

SETTING THE SCENE - THE SAILING SHIP ERA

The formation of the company can be traced to 1790, as the Leith & Clyde Shipping Co., possibly only offering a service between these two ports and as this was 32 years prior to the opening of the Caledonian Canal, all vessels had to travel via the Pentland Firth, that notorious stretch of turbulent water. The vessels employed at that time were probably small sailing smacks of around 50/70 tons and the service frequency is unlikely to have been better than weekly.

In 1820 the 'L&C' amalgamated with the Aberdeen, Dundee & Leith Shipping Co., becoming the Aberdeen, Leith, Clyde & Tay Shipping Co., the positioning of 'Aberdeen' at the beginning of the company title presumably reflecting Aberdeen's position as head office and premier port of call, something which has continued until the present day. The word 'Tay' was apparently soon dropped as it was perhaps an area which did not figure greatly in the company's activity, and the name which came to be used for some 50 years was the Aberdeen,

Leith & Clyde Shipping Co. which was certainly in use by 1824. This was normally shortened to 'AL&C' and interestingly it was still possible in the 1960s to find saloon silverware embossed thus. Examples are on display in the Aberdeen Maritime Museum.

Little is known of the early vessels but the *Glasgow Packet* was built in 1811 and the *Edinburgh Packet* (simply *Edinburgh* in some accounts) in 1812. Both built by A. Hall & Co. of Aberdeen, renowned builders of the Aberdeen clippers. The *Glasgow Packet* was about 82 tons, somewhat larger than other ships. This early pair presumably operated on the routes signified by their names. For the first three decades of its existence the 'AL&C' operated only sailing vessels and a further four decades elapsed before sail finally disappeared from the scene.

By 1824 the 'AL&C' had four main routes and a fleet of eight ships, three each allocated to the Leith and Glasgow routes and one each to the Liverpool and Rotterdam routes. The frequencies were 4/5 days, weekly, monthly and six-weekly respectively. The known vessels in the fleet at this time were the

*Stromness pictured after the end of the Second World War with the **St. Ola** (I) and **St. Rognvald** (II). (Ferry Publications Library)*

Above: The **St. Magnus** *(I) was built as the* Waverley *in 1864 for the Silloth-Belfast route of the Northern British Railway. Some three years later she joined the Aberdeen, Leith and Clyde fleet and became both the first vessel to be given the 'Saint' name and their first paddle - steamer. (Ferry Publications Library)*

Left: The paddle steamer **Sovereign** *entering Aberdeen harbour. She was built in 1836 and was disposed of in 1865. (Ferry Publications Library)*

Clyde, the *London* (or *London Packet*) and the *Marquis of Huntly* serving Leith, the *Rotterdam Packet* and the *Liverpool Packet* serving their namesake ports, and the *Edinburgh*. Fares in the cabin were 15/- (75p), 21/- (£1.05), 2.5 Gns. (£2.62½) and 3 Gns. (£3.15) respectively, substantial amounts at that time.

The Liverpool service ceased around 1830/32, while the Glasgow route continued for at least another 12 years and these services may have latterly operated via the Caledonian Canal as it had been opened in 1822. The Rotterdam service has not been traced after 1835 but in 1843 there were still seven smacks trading to Leith and Glasgow and, curiously, the *Belmont*, recorded as serving Grangemouth. One of the Glasgow traders was apparently the *Glasgow Packet* (II), or at least her listed tonnage was quoted as less than before, suggesting a replacement vessel of the same name had been introduced at some stage.

Some seventeen sailing vessels have been identified as belonging to the 'AL&C' but there were possibly others. While sail and steam overlapped in the fleet for some 40 years (1821-1860) the earliest steamers did not operate in the winter months, the Leith route reverting to sail during the winters up to 1937/38 and the long vulnerable Lerwick route up to 1860. Lerwick was served by the *Marquis of Huntly* (formerly serving Leith) in 1828, the *Aberdeen Packet* in 1838/39 and 1843, the *William Hogarth* between 1848 and 1852 and the *Fairy* from 1852 to 1860. This last named was probably the largest sailing vessel in the fleet, a topsail schooner of 150 tons and approximating in tonnage to the first two steamers in the fleet.

EARLY STEAM DAYS

Henry Bell's *Comet* is universally acknowledged as the precursor of powered vessels in UK waters and the first Clyde steamer when she introduced sailings in 1812 between Glasgow, Greenock and Helensburgh, though she did make one foray that year to the West Highlands via the Crinan Canal. The other great Scottish estuary, the Forth, also introduced steamer sailings between Grangemouth and Newhaven (Edinburgh) in 1813, again with the

Comet which had transferred to the east coast, and when she eventually returned to the west coast in 1819 she became the first West Highland steamer. The Tay was the next area to feel the influence of steam when the *Union* commenced plying on the Dundee to Fife (Woodhaven or Newport-on-Tay) ferry crossing in 1821.

All major Scottish estuarial and island areas thus had steamer services, if in some cases very minimal, in place within nine years of the introduction of steam navigation and, in the case of the Clyde, some 42 steamboats had been built to work that area by 1820. Open seas were a rather different matter but in 1821 the Leith & Aberdeen Steam Yacht Co. placed the *Tourist* on the route linking the two named ports, her maiden voyage taking place on 24th May. The *Tourist* called at eight intermediate calling places and took around 12/13 hours for the passage, departing from the terminal ports on alternate days.

The 'AL&C' at this time were operating two trips weekly between Aberdeen and Leith with their vessels and anticipating a loss of trade to the steamer ordered a paddle steamer for their operations. This was the *Velocity*, built by Denny's of Dumbarton and engined by the Greenhead Foundry. The *Velocity* was 149 gross tons and 112 feet long (deck) and was bigger than nearly all the Clyde steamers of the period. She arrived in Aberdeen on 2nd July 1821 from the Clyde and made her maiden voyage two days later to Leith. The terminal used was actually the Stone Pier at Newhaven which was about one mile from the harbour at Leith. Both competing companies' steamers always appear to have berthed at Newhaven but the smacks normally berthed in Leith.

The *Velocity* made the passage south on Mondays,

*The distinctive-looking **Queen** (II) at Victoria Pier, Lerwick. She was the first screw steamer in the fleet, entering service in 1861 and replacing the wrecked **Duke of Richmond**. (Ferry Publications Library)*

Wednesdays and Fridays, returning on Tuesdays, Thursdays and Saturdays, departing at 06.00 daily and calling at Stonehaven, Montrose, Arbroath, Crail, Anstruther, Elie and Dysart. The *Tourist* operated on a similar basis but always sailing in the opposite direction to the *Velocity*. Both companies appear to have charged similar fares of 21/- (£1.05) cabin and 12/- (60p) steerage for the single passage, considerably more than on the ships, while intermediate ports were charged on a pro rata basis. At none of the intermediate ports did the steamer go alongside, passengers being transferred by a small boat, a procedure which must have been exciting, if not actually perilous, on occasions.

The 'L&ASY Co.' ordered a second vessel for the trade from the yard of James Lang of Dumbarton. It was intended that she would supplement the *Tourist*'s sailings and continue on to Inverness via intermediate ports. The new vessel, the *Brilliant*, was launched on 9th June 1821 and was 159 gross tons and 125 feet long (deck). Her maiden voyage commenced from Newhaven at 05.00 on 21st August and appears to have been a direct sailing to Aberdeen before continuing to Peterhead where she lay overnight. The following day calls were made at Fraserburgh, Banff, Portsoy, Cullen, Lossiemouth, Findhorn, Nairn, Cromarty, Fortrose and Fort George, arriving at Inverness at 20.30. The return voyage was made in two similar daily passages on 24th/25th August.

Whichever way the company had intended to operate their two ships, the *Tourist* was withdrawn for refitting at Leith on 7th August 1821, after which she took up the Leith-London service in mid-September. She appears to have operated thus for a further year, after which she was sold to the London

& Edinburgh Steam Packet Co. who maintained that service thereafter.

The *Brilliant* probably made a further trip to Inverness the following week, after which both companies terminated operations for the season. For many years services operated during the summer only, from about April to early October. The 'AL&C' always substituted their smacks on the service during the winter months but also kept some of them operating alongside the *Velocity* during the summer to maintain cargo services.

The *Velocity* and the *Brilliant* both re-entered service in April 1822 after having improvements made to their accommodation. Services had been curtailed to two round trips by each vessel per week and the Inverness visits were not attempted that year as possibly the services previously offered had been unduly generous. Dysart had been dropped from the schedules but both ships were billed to make the Aberdeen to Newhaven passage every Friday, one of the few occasions when they were offering a concurrent service.

The 'L&ASY Co.' altered their schedule at the end of May operating their two Aberdeen trips within the period Monday to Thursday and inaugurating a return Newhaven to Dundee service, outwards on Friday and returning on Saturday. The 'AL&C' possibly saw an opportunity here for they reintroduced a three trip weekly schedule for the *Velocity* at the beginning of June which reverted to the usual two trips in the first week of September. The *Brilliant* came off service in mid-September being chartered by the Government and the *Velocity* was withdrawn in early October.

The succeeding years saw similar schedules operated, the 06.00 start being a regular feature for a considerable period. There were no further experiments as both companies stuck to their twice-weekly service between Aberdeen and Newhaven. However, in 1825 both companies attempted territorial expansion, the 'L&ASY Co.' operated a fortnightly Inverness service during July and August and both companies made one trip to Wick, presumably to test the market.

SERVICE EXTENDED TO KIRKWALL

In February 1826 the *Brilliant* was offered for sale due to the expiry of the agreement between the owning partners. The 'AL&C' stepped in and bought her, probably to forestall any further competition. Since then, until modern times, the company has never experienced any serious major competition. Only the basic service was operated in 1826 while in 1827 the *Brilliant* made two trips to Inverness and one to Wick. The service to Inverness was organised on a permanent basis in 1829 operating weekly during the summer period. Wick still had an occasional steamer but received a permanent service in 1833, but only fortnightly initially and only during the summer. The Wick steamer this year also extended her run to Kirkwall on a permanent basis after having made a test run the previous year.

The company was now operating the three services (Newhaven, Inverness and Wick/Kirkwall) with the two original steamers and the provision of additional tonnage was becoming imperative. In 1836, therefore, the *Sovereign* appeared, at 378 tons more than twice the tonnage of the earlier pair. The *Sovereign* introduced the system of giving the ships names with a monarchical flavour, this nomenclature being employed for 25 years. The year 1836 was a significant year in that the Wick/Kirkwall service became weekly and was also extended to Lerwick, initially on an alternate week basis. After a decade

cautiously experimenting in northern waters and gradually increasing services, 1836 marked the year of the origins of P&O Scottish Ferries' service pattern, before NorthLink took over the operations to Orkney. Some 162 years later, the *St. Sunniva* (III) operations allowed for a departure from Aberdeen (Saturday); Stromness (Saturday/Sunday); Lerwick (Sunday/Monday); and Aberdeen (Tuesday). This service was a direct successor of the 1836 *Sovereign* route departing from Aberdeen (Friday); Wick (Saturday); Kirkwall (Saturday); Lerwick (Sunday/Monday); Kirkwall (Tuesday); Wick (Tuesday); Aberdeen (Tuesday). With the discontinuation of Wick and the substitution of Stromness for Kirkwall this altered little until 2002, although the *Sovereign* always commenced and terminated her sailings at Newhaven. In 1838 the company obtained the mail contract and have continued to provide mail services ever since.

Eventually, trade also justified keeping the service running in the winter months. This probably commenced in 1838 for the Aberdeen to Newhaven service as an additional vessel, the *Duke of Richmond*, slightly larger than the *Sovereign*, was built that year. Winter services were introduced in 1848 for Inverness, 1850 for Wick and 1858 for the islands. In 1840/41, the Edinburgh terminal had been moved from Newhaven to Granton, about a mile further west.

Services were basically unchanged in the period 1836 to 1859 though there were a number of fleet changes. The *Brilliant* was lost when wrecked on the North Pier at Aberdeen in 1839 and replaced by the three-year-old *Bonnie Dundee* in 1840. The *Velocity* was sold in 1844 and replaced by the *Queen* (I), having been built for the company. Fleet strength was maintained at four vessels most of this time but two additional vessels were acquired in 1849. The

*The **St. Magnus** (I) (ex **Waverley**) at Lerwick. (A. Deayton collection)*

first was the two-year-old *Newhaven* from the
Brighton & Continental Steam Packet Co., a thinly
disguised 'cover' name for the London Brighton &
South Coast Railway Co., who operated a cross-
Channel service, but she was only retained for a year
and a half and then sold in 1851. The other vessel
was the *Hamburg*, built for the company as their first
iron ship, but she was herself sold in 1852.
Generally, services could be maintained by three
vessels, so a fleet of four was probably adequate to
cover overhaul etc. and so an increase to six in the
years between 1849 and 1852 appears curious.

After thirteen years with the company the *Bonnie
Dundee* was sold in 1853, thus reducing the fleet once
again to three vessels and it appears that it was in
this year that Aberdeen to Granton sailings as a
separate service ceased, though of course the
northern sailings invariably commenced at Granton,
Aberdeen being effectively an intermediate port of
call. It is unclear when the intermediate places
between Aberdeen and Granton ceased to be ports of
call and as the section between Arbroath and
Aberdeen was finally rail-connected in 1850 they
probably fell victim to this new mode of transport at
that time. The ports along the Fife coast section were
progressively rail-connected between 1863 and 1883
but by the early 1850s there were other competing
steamboat owners operating in the Firth of Forth
and they had probably taken over the local traffic by
then. For most, if not all, of the period 1821 to
c.1850 the intermediate calling places on the east
coast remained as Stonehaven, Montrose, Arbroath,
Crail, Anstruther and Elie, although Johnshaven
(between Stonehaven and Montrose) was employed
from 1824 to c.1831 and possibly later, and Largo
(west of Elie) was mentioned in 1853. Dysart may
have been dropped at the end of the first (1821)
season but is also mentioned in 1853. One other
vessel joined the fleet in 1847, the smallest ever
owned by the company. This was the tug *Victory* and
her main function appears to have been to tender to
the other vessels as and when required. She was
stationed in Aberdeen and apart from tendering to
vessels lying in the harbour she apparently also
carried out this function on occasions when 'AL&C'
vessels lay off Aberdeen instead of entering,
presumably when tidal conditions or commercial
considerations so dictated.

From 1850 an additional sailing was provided to
Wick and this was extended to Scrabster in 1852.
This was the start of the Caithness route, a service
which operated for over 100 years and on its
introduction it was usual for the Wick call to be
dropped from the 'indirect' steamer's itinerary
during the winter months. 'Indirect' in this context
referred to the Aberdeen-Wick-Kirkwall-Lerwick
route as opposed to the 'direct' Aberdeen-Lerwick
route which only commenced in 1891. For virtually
all its existence the Caithness steamer left Granton

on a Monday or Tuesday, calling at Aberdeen the
same day and after making the north calls returning
to Granton on Thursday evenings.

The very early steamers were in the 150 to 400
ton range but the *Duke of Richmond* was around 500
tons and the *Hamburg* was almost 700 tons. Apart
from the coastal east coast sailings the usual pattern
up to 1859 saw departures from Newhaven/Granton
on Mondays for Caithness, Tuesdays for Inverness,
the usual calling ports (thought not necessarily every
trip) being Banff, Cullen, Lossiemouth, Burghead,
Cromarty, Invergordon, and Fort George. The
Friday sailing was to Wick, Kirkwall and Lerwick and
normally all sailings called at Aberdeen in both
directions. The Inverness service was terminated in
1859, no doubt due to the fact that Aberdeen and
Inverness were rail linked in 1858 but strangely it
was reintroduced in 1874 for one year only.

The *Queen* (I) was lost when she struck the Carr
Rock off Fife Ness on 19th April 1857 and the *Duke
of Richmond* was another loss on 8th October 1859
when she became stranded on the Aberdeenshire
shore about one-and-a-half miles north of the River
Don. To compensate, the new *Prince Consort* joined
the fleet in March 1858 while the *Hamburg* was re-
purchased from her Grimsby owners in 1860.
However, fleet strength was down to two vessels for
much of the period 1857 to 1860 and a number of
chartered vessels were employed to assist, this being
the first occasion that chartering was recorded. They
included the *Commodore* (1857/58); the *Earl of
Aberdeen* (1857/58); and the *Duke of Rothesay* (1858).
All three came from the Aberdeen Steam Navigation
Co. who operated the Aberdeen to London service.

To reinstate the fleet to four vessels the *Queen* (II)
was built in September 1861 and was effectively a
replacement for the *Duke of Richmond* which had
been lost two years earlier. The *Queen* (II) was
noteworthy in that she was the first screw steamer in
the fleet. The *Hamburg* was wrecked on Scotston
Head in October 1862 and the *Prince Consort* was
seriously damaged in May 1863 when she struck the
North Pier at Aberdeen. She was sold in that
condition, the purchaser reconstructing her and
selling her back to the 'AL&C' later the same year.
Initially the *Dundee* was chartered from the Dundee,
Perth & London Co. to provide cover as this mishap
had reduced the fleet to two vessels. Another
paddler, the *Vanguard*, was later purchased from the
Steam Packet Co. of Dublin to temporarily fill the
gap and she brought ship strength up to three
initially, and to four once the *Prince Consort* rejoined
the fleet. Unfortunately the *Prince Consort* was herself
wrecked on the Altens Rock, a couple of miles south
of Aberdeen, on 11th May 1867 and as this left the
'AL&C' with only two vessels once again, the *Princess
Alice* was chartered from the Aberdeen & Newcastle
Shipping Co. until a replacement could be found,
while the *Dundee* (Dundee, Perth & London Co.) was

Above: The deck saloon on board the **St. Magnus** *(I). (Ferry Publications Library)*

Left: The **St. Clair** *(I) entered commercial service in 1868. (Bruce Peter collection)*

also on charter during April and May. The second vessel in the fleet, the *Brilliant* had been lost in 1839. The following two decades were loss-free and the 'AL&C' appears to have been more unfortunate than most in that four vessels, the *Queen* (I), the *Duke of Richmond*, the *Hamburg* and the *Prince Consort* had all been lost through marine peril in the decade 1857 to 1867.

THE NEW DAWN

While the geographical extension of services had followed a slow continuous pattern over the years, the links with the outparts and Aberdeen/Leith, with the possible exception of Wick, had invariably been on the basis of a weekly call at best. All this was to change in 1866 when a second vessel was allocated to the 'indirect' route, known as the 'secondary indirect' vessel. The basic schedule was Granton (Tuesday); Aberdeen (Wednesday); Kirkwall (Wednesday/Thursday); Lerwick (Thursday/Friday); Kirkwall (Friday); Aberdeen (Saturday); Leith (Saturday). The *Queen* (II) was the first vessel allocated to this route. This service appears to have operated only during the summer, though this was modified after 1937 and was continued in one form or another until 1966. The replacement for the *Prince Consort* was the *Waverley*, the first of that name, and originally built in 1864 for the Silloth-Belfast route of the North British Company. Early in 1867 she was overhauled and fitted out on the Tyne and entered north service at the end of that year. She was renamed *St. Magnus* (I), commencing a style of nomenclature still in use some 130 years later. She was also noteworthy in that she was the last paddler to join the fleet, and the only two-funnel vessel ever owned (until the introduction of the ro-ro vessels). At just over 600 tons, she was of similar size to the *Hamburg*, the *Prince Consort* and the *Vanguard* and was generally employed on the 'indirect' route. Presumably to minimise stress on her paddle wheels, she appears never to have done any winter work in her long career and would normally appear in service between mid-March and mid-April and would then be laid up from about the end of October.

The *Vanguard* was sold in 1868 for breaking up and was replaced the same year by the new *St. Clair* (I), the second screw steamer in the fleet. Although slightly greater in tonnage than the *St. Magnus* (I)

she was 20 feet shorter and initially operated the Caithness service, commencing in March of that year.

From 1821 to 1867 some thirteen steamers had joined the 'AL&C' and of them six had been second-hand purchases. Each had averaged nine years with the company. New vessels in that period had averaged 15 years in company service. The introduction of the *St.Clair* (I) in 1868 must have marked a major turning point in the company's economic circumstances as for the next 45 years all vessels built for the 'AL&C' arrived new from the builders. It was only the outset of the 1914-18 war that reversed this trend.

The *St. Clair* (I) was followed in 1871 by the *St. Nicholas*, the only time this name was ever used and one of the few occasions when a 'Saint' name has never been repeated. The *St. Nicholas* took over the Caithness service and she and the *St. Clair* (I) largely shared the route between them until the turn of the century. These vessels were clipper-bowed and were difficult to tell apart, their sterns being their most differentiating feature.

By this time there was a fleet of four ships. The *St. Nicholas* at 787 tons was the largest, the other two Saints being just over the 600 tons, while the *Queen* (I) at 328 tons was the smallest. It was an exceptionally modern fleet in 1871: the *Queen* (10 years), the *St. Magnus* (7 years), the *St. Clair* (3 years), plus the new *St. Nicholas*, the average age profile of 5 years never to be attained again.

THE NORTH COMPANY

In June 1875 the Aberdeen, Leith & Clyde Shipping Co. became the North of Scotland & Orkney & Shetland Steam Navigation Company – usually abbreviated to the 'North Co.'.

*The **St. Rognvald** (I) was built in 1883. She was the first AL & C's ship over 1,000 gross tons and was to inaugurate the Norwegian Fjord cruises in 1886. (Bruce Peter collection)*

In 1881 it was decided that Shetland would receive a third weekly sailing and this was inaugurated by the *Queen* (II) as a seasonal summer sailing that year. There was one major alteration in that after leaving Aberdeen she proceeded to Stromness and Scalloway, rather than Kirkwall and Lerwick, thus servicing the western side of the two island groups. Due to the difficulties in road travel in Shetland, this service also called at various west coast ports including Spiggie, Walls, Brae, Voe, Aith and Hillswick, generally fortnightly in summer and monthly in winter. Hillswick, where the company opened their own St. Magnus Hotel in 1900, was served weekly during the summer. Occasional calls were also made at Reawick or Ronas Voe (an important fishing station during the season) but these did not appear in the timetables. Orkney was not totally neglected as the southbound steamer normally called at St. Margaret's Hope fortnightly after leaving Stromness.

A DECADE OF GROWTH (1882-1892)

From 1836 until 1881 the fleet had always remained at three or four vessels, this sometimes including one or two on charter. The next decade saw fleet size increase to seven by 1887 and nine by 1892. Thereafter it remained at nine or ten until the 1939-45 Second World War. This decade of expansion saw the introduction of a number of new routes and to some extent mirrored the expansion of the Shetland fishing trade.

For about 500 years there has been a ferry crossing between Caithness and Orkney and it was in 1856 that a locally owned Stromness vessel commenced a steamer service between Stromness and Scrabster. In 1874 the Highland railway reached Wick and Thurso. In 1877, having obtained the mail contract, it commenced operating the route, seeing this as a logical extension to their northern main line. When Scapa Pier (two miles from Kirkwall) was opened in 1880, this became the Orkney terminal,

*Above: The Argyll Steamship Company's **Argyll** was chartered during 1891-1892 for the winter direct services. (A. Deayton collection).*

*Right: The **St. Ninian** (I) arriving at Aberdeen. She was built in 1895. Her arrival brought the North Company fleet up to ten vessels. (Ferry Publications Library)*

*The **St. Nicholas** was built in 1871 for the Caithness service and was the only North Company vessel ever to receive this name. (Bruce Peter collection)*

Stromness being relegated to a twice-weekly call. The route was apparently not profitable and the North Company took it over in 1882 building the *St. Olaf* specially for the route. This was the shortest route ever operated by the company and on a daily Monday-Saturday basis. The North Company reinstated Stromness as the home port and Scapa Pier became a daily call in each direction for the uplift and delivery of mail. Hoxa, a headland near St. Margaret's Hope, was a calling place, not always on a daily basis, where passengers were ferried ashore in a small boat.

The *St. Rognvald* (I) joined the fleet in 1883 and at just over 1,000 tons was the largest vessel. She spent most of her career on the main indirect route. She was the first vessel used following the inauguration of the Norwegian cruise programme in 1886, a series of ten-day cruises from Leith and Aberdeen, between 24th June and 24th August. This was such a success that the company built the *St. Sunniva* (I) in 1887, specifically for this role, her appearance was of a large imposing steam yacht. The *St. Sunniva* was the first purpose-built cruise vessel in the world and the first company vessel to be built with the relatively new triple expansion engine. Thereafter the subsequent steamships built for the company were fitted out with the same engines.

The Norwegian cruising season usually operated from late May until mid-September and encompassed the Norwegian coast and fjords between Stavanger in the south to Trondheim to the north. A steam launch was carried (also on the *St. Rognvald*) to ferry passengers ashore at the various ports of call and on certain shore excursions it allowed passengers to re-embark at a different location from their landing point. The *St. Sunniva* cruises were so popular that the *St. Rognvald* had to be enlisted to take the overflow for the two July cruises in the first year. Henceforth, the *St. Rognvald* was incorporated into the advertised cruising programme every year, apart from in 1890, but her absence from the regular routes meant that the North Company had to charter tonnage for their own domestic services. The *Ethel* (from MacBrayne's) was employed during July/August 1889 and the *Quiraing* (McCallum & Co.) from June to August 1891. The summer tonnage shortage was only cured when the *St. Giles* (I) joined the fleet in 1892.

There was further expansion in the Norwegian cruising in 1888 when the *St. Sunniva* and the *St. Rognvald* were rescheduled for the summer season so that their earlier ten-day cruises were extended to 12 days duration and allowed for a regular fortnightly departure from Leith/Aberdeen and weekly when

*Above: A rare picture of the short-lived **St. Magnus** (II). She was sunk off Peterhead in 1918. (Ferry Publications Library)*

*Right: The **St.Rognvald** (II) leaving Leith. (Bruce Peter collection)*

both vessels operated. The *St. Rognvald* had a slightly shorter season than the *St. Sunniva*. This eventually allowed for Saturday departures from Leith/Aberdeen to Stavanger with Tuesday departures from Bergen ten days later for the return voyage. The first sailing for the 1888 season was for a 21-day North Cape cruise undertaken by the *St. Rognvald* and the final sailing advertised for the *St. Sunniva* was for a Baltic cruise which did not operate. In subsequent years the programme included one cruise to each of these destinations and in 1898 both vessels made a Baltic cruise, the *St. Rognvald* in May/June and the *St. Sunniva* in August/September. An unusual feature of the cruising programme was that passengers could break their journey at any of the ports of call, returning by the following or any subsequent sailing.

Reverting to 1877, a company called the Shetland Islands Steam Navigation Company had been formed to provide a steamer service between Lerwick and the north isles of Shetland with the *Earl of Zetland* (I). Fifty per cent of this company appears to have been owned by the North Company and was fully absorbed by them in 1890. This brought another route into the North Company's operations as inter-island sailings continued as before. At 253 tons gross (186 prior to its lengthening in 1884) the *Earl of Zetland* was very much the 'baby' of the fleet, about half the tonnage of the *Queen* (II).

DIRECT SERVICES TO SHETLAND

The next and final new route to be introduced to the company's schedules was the 'direct' route from Leith/Aberdeen to Lerwick with no intermediate calls. This was inaugurated by the *St. Nicholas* in the summer of 1891 and was virtually unique to the main services. It operated twice-weekly departing Aberdeen on Mondays and Thursdays and leaving from Lerwick on Tuesdays and Saturdays, spending

the weekends in Leith. During the winter months the route was reduced to one round trip weekly. Perhaps due to the winter overhaul programme, the route was covered by the chartered *Argyll* (Argyll Steamship Company) during the first winter. The *St. Giles* (I) was built in 1892 and appears to have been used solely for this route during her short career of ten years. At 407 tons gross (later lengthened 23 feet making 465 tons) she was the smallest of the main service liners.

The *St. Olaf* also had a very short career on the Pentland Firth from 1882-1890 and, reputedly underpowered, was sold to Canadian interests. For two years a variety of vessels serviced the route with the *John o' Groats* (McCallum & Co.), the *Argyll* (Argyll Steamship Co.), the *Express* (G. Robertson) and the company's own *Queen* (II) also taking spells of duty. The final vessel during this decade was the *St. Ola* (I) which commenced service on the Pentland Firth route in 1892. It should be noted that *St. Ola* is the Orkney variation of the *St. Olaf*, hence the change in the ship's name.

Two ships were converted to triple expansion machinery, the *St. Olaf* in 1890 and the *St. Nicholas* in 1891, but strangely the *St. Rognvald* (I) was not included where fuel savings could have been much greater in her case. By 1892 the nine ships in the fleet included four which were no more than nine years old, although the other five ranged between fifteen and thirty-one years old, giving an average of 15 years overall. The routes operated provided a pattern which was to exist, albeit with some adjustments, until 1956 when the Caithness service

Above: The **St. Nicholas** *aground off Wick, c.1902. (Ferry Publications Library)*

ceased, or 1975 if the Shetland north isles routes are taken as the cut-off point. The present ro-ro routes retain recognisable similarities with those other services operated over a century ago.

CONSOLIDATION

This next period of change by the North Company was their withdrawal from the Norwegian cruise trade and replacing older ships with others which were larger and equipped to a higher standard, improving facilities for passengers and providing greater cargo capacity.

The first new vessel was the *St. Ninian* (I) in 1895. She had spells on most of the main routes, but she was particularly associated with the secondary indirect route for most of her lengthy career. She was effectively an able and sound vessel, bringing the fleet up to ten ships.

On 24th April 1900, on her usual passage from Lerwick to Kirkwall (main indirect service), the *St. Rognvald* (I) ran aground in thick fog on Burgh Head, Stronsay. While all the passengers were safely taken off by the lifeboats, all the livestock was lost. Her deckhouse was subsequently salvaged and now serves as a summer house in a Kirkwall garden.

Unlike their northern routes where the company had a near monopoly of services, the Norwegian cruising season had attracted quite a few competitors. Both Currie's Castle Line and the Union Steamship Company (prior to their 1899 amalgamation) provided a single cruise in 1887. Wilson's of Hull (from 1886) and Salvesen's of Leith (from 1887) provided regular North Sea

crossings/cruises and numerous others were attracted to the scene. Presumably this competition played a part in the North Company's decision to restrict their own Norwegian cruises to a single ship operation following the loss of the *St. Rognvald* (I). After the loss of *St. Rognvald* (I) the *St. Sunniva's* programme dropped her longer distance cruises to the North Cape and the Baltic apart from a Baltic cruise operated in the 1900 season. The programme now consisted of seven fjord cruises followed by the round-Britain cruise lasting about three months at the end of the season. A single fjord cruise in 1902 commenced at Tilbury, apparently the only occasion that this was offered. However, the Norwegian cruising programme was obviously feeling the effects of competition, especially from those companies operating larger ships with better facilities. The Orient Line's *Chinburay* had made a trip from London in 1889 and was joined by the *Garonne* for the July/August season in 1891. In 1907 the North Company only operated six Norwegian cruises while the 1908 season was cut back to two months, although two round-Britain cruises were provided that year, the first cruise sailing anti-clockwise – probably the first time that had ever occurred. Innovation was not entirely lacking and in 1901 the *St. Sunniva* provided a round-Britain cruise at the end of her Norwegian cruising season proceeding from Leith to Gravesend where the cruise had commenced. This appears to have been repeated every season thereafter. While calls varied from year to year, Torquay, Dartmouth, Plymouth, Isle of Man, Greenock, Oban and Stornoway were usually visited and calls were occasionally made at Dublin, Rothesay and Skye. At least one call was usually made at Stromness, Kirkwall and Lerwick on these cruises,

*Above: The first purpose-built cruise vessel was the **St. Sunniva** (I). She is seen here in the Norwegian Fjords. (Ferry Publications Library)*

*Right: The **St. Sunniva** (I) was converted to a mail steamer in 1908. (Ferry Publications Library)*

something which rarely occurred on the Norwegian sailings. The year of 1908 saw the end of the Norwegian cruising programme after 23 years. The *St. Sunniva* (I) was converted to a more conventional mail steamer and took over the direct route between Leith/Aberdeen and Lerwick, rarely deviating from this service.

A replacement, the *St. Rognvald* (II), entered service in 1901 and was the second vessel to exceed the 1,000 ton mark. For her first 24 years she was generally operated on the main indirect service. The *St. Giles* (I) was wrecked when she ran aground near Rattray Head lighthouse (between Fraserburgh and Peterhead) in thick fog on 28th September 1902. She was replaced by the *St. Giles* (II) in 1903 which was placed on the direct route. The *St. Magnus* (I) was sold the same year to Gibraltar interests and whatever perceived failings were attributed to her, she was a most competent vessel during her 36 years with the North Company. Following the disposal of the *Vanguard* in 1868, the *St. Magnus* (I) had been the sole paddler in the fleet. Though little used in the winter periods, she appears to have suffered little from paddle wheel failures and had generally operated a 'long' season, approximately March/April to the end of October. This was curtailed by about a month in the early part of the season from the early 1890s, but from 1896/97 she normally provided the twice-weekly direct service when she was replaced by the new *St. Rognvald* (II). Her final two years were essentially as 'spare' vessel, being in operation for about nine weeks in 1902 and only four weeks in 1903. She managed a further ten years on Mediterranean service, running between Gibraltar and Tangier before going to Dutch breakers.

Another innovation for the company was a Mediterranean cruise from London in March 1896, the majority of passengers joining either at Marseilles (on 1st April) or Naples the following day. Lengthy calls were made at Piraeus, Constantinople, Jaffa and Alexandria, returning to Naples on 1st May and Marseilles two days later.

One further vessel remains to be mentioned, the *St. Fergus*, built for the company in 1913. This was a small cargo coaster, the first in the fleet, and her

intended role is somewhat obscure as she was sold before completion to an Argentinian company.

WAR AND AFTERMATH (1914-1924)

When the First World War commenced the fleet consisted of eight vessels. The ninth, the *St. Nicholas*, had been lost in June of that year. This was adequate in that five vessels could maintain the main routes with one each allocated to the North Isles and the Pentland Firth, allowing one to be spare. However, during the period 1909 to 1914, two ships had been allocated to the direct route during the summer, reducing the service to one in the winter.

Activities during the war are relatively obscure, although the *St. Ninian* (I) served as a naval ferry for most of the conflict, sailing between Scrabster and Scapa Flow. Three ships, the *Sunniva* (I), the *St. Magnus* (II) and the *St. Margaret* were all chartered out for periods, under the control of G & J Burns Ltd. Perhaps due to this factor, three cargo ships were purchased in 1916, one being the erstwhile *St. Fergus* which, at last, sailed under the company's house flag. The *Temaire* was bought from James McKelvie of Glasgow but only remained with the company for a year before being sold again. The third of this trio was the *Cape Wrath* from the Cape Steam Shipping Company of Glasgow.

Three ships were lost during the war, all within a ten-month period. The first was the *Express* which had earlier served on charter on the Pentland Firth for periods between 1890 and 1892. She had been the fourth wartime ship to be purchased in 1917 but was lost in a collision off the French coast in April of that year, achieving the dubious distinction of having the shortest career of any North Company vessel. What she was doing so far from 'home' is unknown, but she could have conceivably been a supply vessel for the British Army in France. On 12th September 1917 the *St. Margaret*, on passage from Lerwick to Iceland, was torpedoed thirty miles east of the Faroes and sank rapidly with the loss of five of her crew. Her master was Captain William Leask who sailed 150 miles to Shetland in a lifeboat with eighteen of his crew landing at Hillswick after three days. Captain Leask was later in command of the *St. Clair* (I) when she was attacked by a submarine off Fair Isle on 19th January 1918, when two of the crew were killed. The attackers were driven off and Captain Leask received the DSC for this action. The final loss was the *St. Magnus* (II) due to enemy action off Peterhead on 12th February 1918 while on a passage from Lerwick to Aberdeen. Two passengers and one crew member were lost at that time.

The company made a fifth purchase in 1918 when the *Cape Wrath* was obtained from G & J Burns and renamed the *Ape*, though the change in the name style has never been explained. She was lost post-war after striking rocks in St. Malo Roads on 13th April 1919, suggesting that her role may have been as a replacement for the *Express*.

At the end of the war the fleet stood at nine, one more than in 1914, but there were some major changes. Three of the fleet were now small cargo coasters and there were only four main line service vessels, the youngest, the *St. Rognvald*, being 17 years old and with the average age of this quartet being 30 years. With the loss of their two newest vessels, the average age of the fleet was 26 years, five years more than when the conflict started.

The conditions in the post-war depression years meant that there was no new-build programme. The loss of the *Fetlar* (I) was made good by the purchase of the 36-year-old *Cavalier* from MacBraynes in 1919, which was renamed the *Fetlar* (II). She only

remained in the fleet for a year and spent part of her service on the north isles route. A second purchase from MacBrayne's, also in 1919, was their *Chieftain* which was renamed the *St. Margaret* (II) and was employed on the west side service. Passenger services were curtailed immediately after the war mainly because the *St. Ninian* did not reappear from her post-war reconditioning until the winter of 1919. The 1919 summer programme consisted only of the direct (once-weekly), the main indirect and west side services. There was no secondary indirect service or Caithness steamer. Services were nearer normality in 1920 but the *St. Sunniva*, although reverting to twice-weekly service between Aberdeen and Lerwick, did not call at Leith. This may have been due to the inflationary cost of coal and numerous strikes at this period, or to the shortage of experienced officers. The Caithness service was not fully restored until the 1921 season.

From 1921 the allocation of main line service vessels was:

Direct	*St. Sunniva* (I)
Main Indirect Direct	*St. Rognvald* (II)
Secondary Indirect	*St. Ninian* (I)
West side	*St. Margaret* (II)
Caithness	*St. Clair* (I)

The *St. Ola* and the *Earl of Zetland* operated on the minor routes with the *Cape Wrath* and *St. Fergus*

*The distinctive-looking **St. Sunniva** (I). Her cruises ended in 1908 after which she was converted to a mail steamer. This view shows her probably pictured off Aberdeen following her conversion for the Lerwick service in 1908. She was lost in April 1930 after grounding on Mousa. All passengers and crew got ashore safely but bad weather prevented the vessel from being salvaged. (Ferry Publications Library)*

*Above: A busy scene at Lerwick harbour during the busy summer herring period with the **St. Sunniva** (I) just about to leave the berth for her direct run to Aberdeen. The **Earl of Zetland** (I) and **St. Rognvald** (II) can be seen on the left of the dock. (Ferry Publications Library)*

*Right: The **St. Rognvald** (II) arriving at Leith after the Second World War. She was not broken up until 1951, after 50 years of service. (Ferry Publications Library).*

looking after cargo commitments. As the secondary indirect route was a summer-only service, there was always a spare vessel to cover winter overhauls.

BETWEEN THE WARS (1924-1939)

The economic climate had been improving during the early part of the 1920s as the *St. Magnus* (III) joined the fleet in 1924, the first new-build ship since the two in 1912/13. She replaced the *St. Margaret* (II) which was sold to Canada in 1925 after only six years in the fleet and had a long and honourable career in British Columbia until 1945. The arrival of the *St. Magnus* (III) marked a considerable increase in the size of the main line vessels. Apart from the two *St. Giles* vessels, virtually all the main line steamers from 1868 had been between 700 and 1,100 tons gross. The *St. Magnus* (III) was relatively massive at almost

1,600 tons gross and with considerable passenger accommodation, originally 234 berths in the First Class and 84 in the Second Class, a combined total which was not to be exceeded until the introduction of the ro-ro ferries some 50 years later. While many of the cabins were 2/4 or 4-berth, the original configuration included two 16-berth cabins and one 8/18-berth cabin which was in the First Class area! Strangely there were no 2-berth cabins and Second Class passengers were restricted to two 42-berth cabins. The three main public rooms in the First Class section were also adaptable in that the settee seating around the sides was convertible to an upper and lower bunk configuration and by this means it added 16 berthed passengers in the smoking room, 16 in the winter dining saloon and 24 in the summer

*Above: The **St. Ola** (I) departing from Stromness. The steamer enjoyed a remarkable 59-year career (1892-1951) on the Pentland Firth. (Ferry Publications Library).*

*Right: Landing at Hoxa from the **St. Ola** (I) in Androo's boat. The 'flit-boat' was the usual method of disembarkation at the islands without suitable piers. (Ferry Publications Library)*

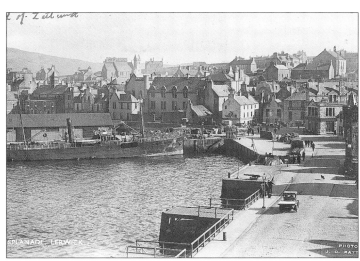

*Above: The **Earl of Zetland** (I) at the North side of the Victoria Pier, Lerwick. She was acquired from Shetland Isles Steam Navigation Company in 1890. (Ferry Publications Library)*

dining saloon helping to accommodate the peak of extra summer passengers. The *St. Magnus* (III) also broke new ground in that she had three hatches and corresponding holds, Numbers 1 and 2 forward, and Number 3 aft. Previous vessels had been provided with single holds fore and aft. These were worked by three steam cranes, all as was customary, mounted on to the starboard side of the ship. The impression of size was further enhanced by the three-deck bridge structure, an innovation giving the wheelhouse etc., officers' accommodation and the smoking room (lounge). In all previous vessels the smoking room, where provided, had been sited at the aft deck house. On the introduction of the *St. Magnus* (III) she was placed on the main indirect route, displacing the *St. Rognvald* (II) to the west side route.

Four years later (1928) the *St. Clement* (I) joined the fleet, replacing the *Cape Wrath* after eleven years

of service. The *St. Clement* (I) was another cargo ship but also innovatory in that she had limited passenger accommodation for twelve in the mid-ship accommodation block. Her main duty was as winter Caithness steamer from approximately mid-October to May, although in the late 1930s she was terminating about a month earlier. Her other main duty was to relieve the *Earl of Zetland* (I) for approximately three to four weeks generally during late September-early October, she had only a limited passenger certificate for this duty. During early September she normally spent two to three weeks as a seasonal livestock carrier, shipping sheep and cattle from the islands to Aberdeen. For the remainder of the summer she varied her activities between coping with 'overflows' on the main routes and acting as a general tramping coaster, frequently loading coal cargoes from Granton, Burntisland, Blyth, Seaham, Amble etc. to various destination ports, not necessarily in the northern islands, work which was

*Left: This stern view of the **St. Rognvald** (II) shows her with a yellow funnel. (Ferry Publications Library)*

*Above: The **St. Catherine** (I) (ex **Lairdsbank**, ex **Lairds Olive**) approaching Scalloway during summer 1930. (Ferry Publications Library)*

very much the domain of the *St. Fergus*. Her trading area extended from Stornoway to Hamburg and London.

LOSS OF THE ST. SUNNIVA

In 1930 the North Company experienced their final peace-time ship loss when the *St. Sunniva* (I) ran aground on rocks on the island of Mousa on the morning of Thursday, 10th April while on passage to Lerwick. All passengers were saved but the ship broke up and sank two weeks later. Her bell was salvaged in recent years and is now displayed in Lerwick Museum. Coming so soon and prior to the beginning of the summer season with only four main line steamers out of the necessary five, a replacement was needed quickly. This took the form of the *Lairdsbank* (formerly *Laird's Olive* of Burns & Laird). She was renamed *St. Catherine* (I) and commenced her service at the beginning of June on the west-side route for that season. The *St. Magnus* (III) became the direct steamer and the *St. Rognvald* (II) reverted to the main indirect route.

The *St. Catherine* (I) was obviously a stop-gap and a new ship the *St. Sunniva* (II) entered service at the beginning of June 1931. In many ways the *St. Sunniva* (II) was an anachronism as she perpetuated the clipper bow and figurehead of many of her predecessors and with her white hull, yacht lines and yellow funnel, could easily have been mistaken for a large steam yacht, although the two steam cranes betrayed her true role as a coastal passenger steamer. Although dimensionally slightly larger than the *St.*

Magnus (III), her smaller superstructure was largely responsible for her tonnage being about 200 gross tons, less than her immediate predecessor. She had one hundred and twelve First Class berths, less than half the capacity of the *St. Magnus* (III) of which ten were 2-berth cabins. There were fourteen 2/4-berth cabins and a ladies cabin sleeping sixteen. The dining room sat fifty-four and there was a smoking room in the aft deck house. The Second Class gents cabin was able to sleep fifty-four in berths, probably the largest number every provided for, and in addition there were settees which could have accommodated a further sixteen to eighteen. The ladies cabin had berths for eighteen plus settees for four or five. One peculiarity was that the only access to the ladies cabin was by negotiating the gents cabin!

The *St. Sunniva* (II) was placed on the direct route on which she served for virtually all her peace-time service. The *St. Magnus* (III) and *St. Rognvald* (II) reverted to the main indirect and the west-side routes respectively and while the *St. Catherine* (I) was retained for winter operations, it was the company policy to use the *St. Sunniva* (II) for the summer operations only. From her introduction, the *St. Magnus* (III) was originally a summer-only ship (June to September) but did serve on her own route during the winters of 1935/6 and 1936/7 and on the direct routes during the winters of 1937/8 and 1938/9. The winter service on the direct route became a regular duty for the *St. Catherine* (I) and there was the unusual arrangement whereby the

*Above: The **St. Giles** (II) of 1903. Like her predecessors of the same name she enjoyed a brief ten-year spell of service with the North Company. (Ferry Publications Library)*

*Right: The **St. Sunniva** (II) looked more like a private yacht than a passenger ship. (Bruce Peter collection)*

direct route had two vessels allocated to it – a summer boat and a winter boat. The *St. Catherine* (I) made occasional appearances on the west-side route outside her normal winter duty and also relieved the main indirect service at times. In July/August 1933 she had a short charter to the Aberdeen, Newcastle & Hull Steam Company but otherwise the summers were idle at the lay-up buoys in the Victoria Dock, Aberdeen.

The *St. Clair* (I) finished her season on the Caithness route on Friday 30th October 1936 for a winter lay-up and in December was renamed the *St. Colm*, the first and only time this name was used. This was to release the name for the new *St. Clair* (II), another innovatory ship. She was the first vessel to have a fully mid-ship superstructure, all earlier vessels having deck houses erected on the shelter deck. The biggest change internally was that First Class accommodation was still amidships and Second Class was aft. The only accommodation forward was for deck and engine crew. Dimensionally and in tonnage she was marginally bigger than the *St. Magnus* (III).

The internal layout of the new *St. Clair* (II) was that the dining saloon, which always appears to have been described on the deck plans of earlier vessels as 'saloon' or 'dining saloon' was now described as the 'restaurant'. The saloon was a deck higher than on earlier vessels on the shelter or upper deck at the fore end of the superstructure with numerous windows providing good views of the passing scene. Seating was for 56 in tables for two, four or eight.

Above, on the boat deck, was the lounge and this was encircled on three sides by an observation saloon. Aft on the boat deck was a small bar. On earlier vessels the 'bar' had been a small room which was actually a dispensing compartment. Aft of the saloon and on the deck below were the thirty-six cabins, all 2/4-berth convertibles, making provision for 144 berthed passengers. In the Second Class, the smoking room was at the after end of the aft deck house, while the far end had two 4-berth and two 6-berth cabins, somewhat unusually in connected pairs so that a 4-berth had to be negotiated to enter a 6-berth. The entrance lounge with four settees separated cabins from the smoking room. On the main deck below there were four 4-berth and five 6-berth cabins, also a small dining saloon to seat 14, the first time this had been provided in the Second Class area. This was the first ship where 'overflow' bunks were not provided in First Class public rooms, but it was possible to set up a further ten bunks each in the Second Class smoke room and dining saloon. This gave a total of 86 berths in Second Class.

The *St. Clair* (II) spent her first month in service (May 1937) on the main indirect route, but subsequently transferred to the west-side route which she served for the three summers prior to the outbreak of World War II, though winters were spent on the main indirect route.

On the introduction of the *St. Clair* (II) into service, the 44-year-old *St. Catherine* (II) was dispatched to the breakers in the middle of May 1937. This was followed by the 69-year-old *St. Colm*

*Above: The **St. Sunniva** (II) of 1931 arrives off Lerwick. She was lost with all hands whilst on North Atlantic convoy duties in 1943. (Ferry Publications Library)*

Another distinctive view of the St. Sunniva (II) off Aberdeen. This picture was probably taken during builders' trials in 1931. (Ferry Publications Library)

The St. Magnus (III) departing from Lerwick. The steamer joined the fleet in 1924 and remained in service until the 1960s. (Ferry Publications Library)

*The **St. Rognvald** leaving her berth at Stromness. (Ferry Publications Library)*

at the end of July 1937. Even with the disposal of these two elderly vessels, the remaining nine-strong fleet still included four vessels of between thirty-six and sixty-years-old. It seems possible that with this age profile, the company was considering a rolling programme of replacements, but in the event only one further vessel was ordered and delivered prior to the outbreak of war.

The introduction of the *Earl of Zetland* (II) in August 1939 was as a replacement for her 62-year-old namesake which had been renamed *Earl of Zetland II* – the first occasion this 'II' suffix had been employed by the company. The new *Earl of Zetland* was truly a liner in miniature and was the first diesel-engined vessel in the fleet. All subsequent vessels were similarly engined. On her introduction to service on the North Isles route, her predecessor was laid up in Aberdeen, her future uncertain.

THE SECOND WORLD WAR

The 1939 war can be considered to have arrived in 1938 for the North Company. As early as September that year the *St. Clement* (I) is recorded as having made three trips for naval military purposes: (1) Aberdeen to Flotta with a gun pedestal; (2) Leith to Lyness with (telegraph) poles and motor cars; and (3) Rosyth to Lyness with Admiralty mooring gear. Lyness was the main naval shore base on the island of Hoy for Scapa Flow and Flotta which was the largest adjacent island, both being of great

importance once the conflict started.

Most succeeding months saw the *St. Clement* (I) and the *St. Fergus* similarly employed, generally to Lyness, although Longhope, a few miles from Lyness, also featured. Where it has been recorded, cargoes were listed as machinery, huts, motors, tipping wagons, rails, railway sleepers, iron, and in one case, a special charter. The *St. Ninian* (I) also got in on the act with five trips divided between Lyness and Longhope. Two special sailings were made in

*The Smoking Room of the **St. Sunniva** (II). (Ferry Publications Library)*

Possibly one of the most beautiful vessels to plough the waters to Shetland and Orkney was the **St. Sunniva** *(II). She is seen here early in her career. (Bruce Peter collection)*

The **St. Rognvald** *(II) arriving at Leith. She entered service in 1901 and spent her 24 years generally on the main indirect service. (Bruce Peter collection)*

August 1939 for Scottish Command (the Army), which were probably Territorials' movements. The first was by the *St. Clair* (II), Leith-Lyness-Leith, which she managed to fit into her normal lie-over refit at Leith. A fortnight later the *St. Ninian* (I) operated Leith-Lyness-Scapa (Pier) before reverting to her normal Caithness route. The Lyness traffic had obviously been increasing and in that month the *Naviedale* was chartered to make three Leith-Lyness sailings. In addition, the *St. Rognvald* (II) terminated one of her southbound July sailings in Aberdeen and returned to Kirkwall to bring a contingent of Territorials south for their annual camp, travelling direct to Leith.

Although the war commenced on 3rd September 1939, the company had been monitoring the situation for a few weeks beforehand and there had been an exodus of holidaymakers and visitors from the islands. The first real disruption to normal schedules came when the *St. Sunniva* (II) terminated her service at Leith on 27th August and returned to Aberdeen two days later when she was handed over to the Admiralty. She was followed by the *St. Magnus* (III) which had arrived in Leith on the 30th, returned to Aberdeen and was handed over to the Admiralty on the following day. In addition, the *St. Clair* (II) had not proceeded beyond Scalloway on her sailing from Leith on the 27th, but otherwise provided her normal weekly schedule for that week. The *Earl of Zetland* (II) was reactivated after only eight days of idleness to make a cargo run from Aberdeen to Scrabster to assist the *St. Ola* (I) on the Pentland Firth route which was about to begin the busiest ever period in its history. The withdrawal of two of the main line fleet units necessitated the rescheduling of the remaining vessels and initially the *St. Ninian* (I) took the rescheduled 28th August sailing from Leith in place of the *St. Sunniva* (II) but her next sailing, from Aberdeen on 1st September, was on the main indirect service and this was terminated at Lerwick. She then proceeded direct to Scrabster, arriving on 4th September and was handed over to the Admiralty to become the naval ferry for the Pentland Firth service. The withdrawn *Earl of Zetland* (II) after only a few days on the Firth, returned to Aberdeen on the same day. By the second day of the war, three of the main line fleet had been requisitioned, leaving only the *St. Clair* (II) and the *St. Rognvald* (II) to cope. The *Earl of Zetland* (II) was retained until 2nd October taking cargoes from Aberdeen to Wick, Stromness and Kirkwall, but was then laid up until 26th November, her very limited capacity making her unsuitable, even under the circumstances of the time. The *Naviedale*, joined by the *Rimsdale*, were kept on charter throughout September and October 1939 covering the Caithness route at times, and appearing elsewhere as cargo requirements dictated.

As in the First World War, the purchase of second-

The cargo steamer **Roar Head** *was purchased in 1939 and was to remain in the fleet until 1956. (Ferry Publications Library)*

hand tonnage was restarted to make up fleet numbers and the first of these was the *Highlander*, a passenger cargo vessel, purchased at the beginning of October 1939 from the Aberdeen, Newcastle and Hull Steam Co., a vessel roughly comparable to the *St. Magnus* (III) and which had been laid up at the outbreak of war. A further purchase was the cargo ship *Rora Head* from A. F. Henry & McGregor of Leith at the beginning of December 1939 and somewhat similar to the *St. Clement* (I). Early in 1940 a third purchase was the small coasting steamer *Amelia* (built 1894) and at 357 tons gross was even smaller than the *St. Fergus*. This purchase was of a rather different nature in that she had been owned by Cooper and Company of Kirkwall since 1920, operating a direct Kirkwall to Leith service and the purchase was effectively a takeover of Coopers. To the end of her days Coopers retained their own berths, offices and facilities at Leith and Kirkwall. The *Amelia* remained, with few deviations, on her

The **Earl of Zetland** *(II) was the North Company's first diesel-powered ship. (Ferry Publications Library)*

*Above: The **Earl of Zetland** (II) at Lerwick on 19th August 1939 with the **Earl of Zetland** (I) and the **St. Magnus**. (Ferry Publications Library)*

*Right: The **St. Clair** (II) leaving Leith on her maiden voyage on 29th April 1937. (W. Barrie collection)*

'own' route virtually to the end of her days. Some further problems with tonnage resulted in the Caithness route having to be closed, the final sailing was undertaken by the *St. Fergus* from Leith on 5th April 1940. This was followed by the withdrawal of Scalloway calls as from the Leith sailing on 5th May 1940. The west-side service thereafter proceeded no further than Stromness, though it retained the St. Margaret's Hope calls. The *St. Fergus* was also used when the Scalloway calls were terminated.

During 1939 the attempt was made to continue with the long-standing indirect service, but on five different weeks there was no vessel available. The problem was further confounded in that the round trip was taking on average 8/10 days so that it was unusual to find the same vessel making consecutive sailings. Most sailings employed the *St. Rognvald* (II) or the *St. Clair* (II), but the *Highlander* made two trips. The *St. Ninian* (I) and the *St. Clement* (I) also made one sailing each. There were only four sailings in January and February 1940 and one took 16 days for the round journey from Leith. This was followed by a nine-week gap covering March and April. May was unusual in that five sailings were made, thereafter there were only isolated sailings for the rest of the year. As earlier, Leith-Lerwick direct (June to September 1940), Aberdeen to Lerwick (June to September 1940), Aberdeen to Kirkwall (June to November 1940) sailings were provided by the *St. Rognvald* (II), *Highlander* and *St. Clement* (I). Following her de-requisition by the Admiralty, the *St. Magnus* (III) appeared on her old route with a sailing from Leith on 14th August 1940 but this was followed by a ten-week gap. There were only a further few isolated sailings, all provided by *St. Magnus* (III), the last being on 11th January 1941, after which this service did not resume until 1945.

From November 1940 a major change was that all main services were restricted to a link between two ports and from this date there were separate Leith-Kirkwall and Aberdeen-Kirkwall services. The Lerwick direct service was initially continued with the same vessel, generally loading at both Leith and Aberdeen, and while a twice-weekly schedule could not be maintained, the gaps rarely exceeded a week. Initially sailings were divided between the *St. Rognvald* (II) and the *Highlander*, the latter vessel being replaced by the *St. Magnus* (III) from August 1940. Apart from this, the main services were separated into Leith/Aberdeen to Lerwick and Leith/Aberdeen to Kirkwall sailings, the first of these being effectively a continuation of the direct route. Initially an attempt was made to operate the Kirkwall route twice-weekly and until the beginning of October the *St. Clement* (I) made half the sailings, the rest being shared between the *Earl of Zetland* (II), the *Naviedale*, the *Rimsdale* and the *Highlander*. There was a three-week gap after this, and subsequently sailings were made at about 5/6 six-week intervals on average, but the intervals tended to be erratic in duration. Following the October 'gap' and until mid-August 1940, the bulk of the sailings were operated by the *St. Clair* (II), the *St. Clement* (I) and the *Rora Head*, a few by the *St. Fergus* and only isolated appearances by the *St. Rognvald* (II), the *Highlander*, the *Naviedale*, the *Berriedale* (another charter) and the *St. Magnus* (III). The *Highlander* had been attacked by enemy bombers 10 miles south-east of Aberdeen on 2nd August after leaving Aberdeen while operating the Lerwick to Leith sailings. Managing to shoot down two of them, a part of the wreckage of one was strewn across the afterdeck when it crashed.

*Above: The **St. Clair** (II) arriving at Aberdeen in a storm on 20th November 1950. (Ferry Publications Library)*

For this action, Captain William Gifford received an OBE, two crew members received the BEM and three others, including stewardess Miss Cockburn, were commended. After three weeks repairing damage at Leith she resumed service, but it was thought prudent to change her name and she thus became the *St. Catherine* (II). From late August 1940 the Kirkwall service continued as before, the *St. Catherine* (II) taking half the sailings, the others being shared between the *Rora Head*, the *St. Clement* and the *St. Fergus*. It was while thus employed that the *St. Catherine* (II) (formerly *Highlander*) was attacked once again after leaving Aberdeen on 14th November for Kirkwall. Fate was against her on this occasion and she sunk rapidly with the loss of Captain J.G. Norquoy, thirteen crew (including seven from the engine room) and one passenger after a career of just 13 months with the company.

Initially the Lerwick service during 1939 was attempted as a twice-weekly sailing but this was difficult to maintain, October having a particularly poor service with no sailings after the 2nd until the 31st. Most sailings were provided by the *St. Rognvald* (II), the *St. Clair* (II) and the *Highlander*, with the *St. Ninian* (I), the *St. Clement* (I) and the *St. Fergus* all making appearances. From January 1940 the service tended to be approximately weekly with the *St. Rognvald* (II) and the *Highlander* generally alternating until July, the latter vessel being replaced by the *St. Magnus* (III) thereafter. Two 'strangers' appeared, the *Kildrummy* (possibly a charter) for one trip in August and, from May 1941, the *Blyth* (allotted by Ministry of War Transport) which joined

the *St. Rognvald* (II) and the *St. Magnus* (III) until August 1941 when the joint Leith/Aberdeen sailings terminated.

The *Earl of Zetland II* was reactivated on 2nd October 1939 and returned as second vessel for the Pentland Firth route, this occupying her until 22nd January 1940. She then returned to her old haunts, the north isles of Shetland, for the duration of the war and was normally relieved by the *Earl Sigurd* from Orkney. The new *Earl of Zetland* was requisitioned by Scottish Command and used initially for troop movements from Scrabster and within Scapa Flow. Military control was exercised from Stromness and for the first two months she was a regular visitor to Scapa (Pier), Lyness and less frequently to Longhope and Flotta. Overnight lie-overs were shared between Scrabster and Stromness but occasionally Scapa and St. Margaret's Hope were used. From April 1941 she fell into a fairly regular pattern of leaving Scrabster around 12.00, crossing over to Stromness, often with a call at one of the Scapa Flow ports, and then returning similarly to Scrabster, arriving about 17.00/18.00. From about September the Scrabster departure was brought forward to 09.00/10.00, returning around 15.00/16.00. Scrabster was very much her home port during the war but the Saturday sailing was generally northbound only, providing the weekends at Stromness and resuming service from there on Mondays. The naval ferry the *St. Ninian* (I) was based at HMS *Dunluce Castle*, moored at Scapa Flow, making a return crossing daily from there to Scrabster. She was joined by the *Morialta*, a new ship from the Caledon yard for Australian owners but requisitioned by the Admiralty and apparently managed by the North Company from October 1940.

For the rest of the war four ships were required to operate the Pentland Firth routes while the *St. Ola*

*The **St. Clair** (II) at Leith during her early career. (Bruce Peter collection)*

(I) on the commercial service was normally relieved by the *Earl of Zetland*, which, operating as a military ferry, was relieved by the *St. Ninian* (I). The naval ferry continued as a two-ship operation until June 1945 and when the *Morialta* terminated her service at the end of August 1943 she was replaced by the Faroese steamer the *Tjaldur* which had entered the service from June 1943 and was also managed by the

North Company. In all, some twenty-one vessels made appearances on the Pentland Firth routes, some for only very short periods. Both the 'Earls' and the Great Western Railway's Plymouth tender the *Sir Richard Grenville* had the distinction of serving on commercial, naval and military services. Other vessels which had significant spells on the Pentland Firth were the *Calshot* (Southampton tender) and the

escaped Norwegian coastal steamer *Galtesund*, while another Plymouth tender, the *Sir John Hawkins*, appeared on the military service at times.

To return to September 1939 where the *St. Sunniva* (II) and *St. Magnus* (III) lay at Aberdeen under Admiralty requisition, both later sailed from the port on 8th October, the *St. Sunniva* (II) as an accommodation ship in Scapa Flow and the *St.*

Magnus (III) to Kirkwall Bay where she became a guardship for contraband control. Both were briefly diverted in April 1940 for a troopship voyage from Aberdeen to Norway, the third ship in the convoy being Bank Line's *Cedarbank* which was torpedoed and sunk off the Norwegian coast. The *St. Magnus* (III) had a number of other diversions from her static role in Kirkwall Bay and on some of these her place on duty was taken by the *St. Sunniva* (II). On 15th May 1940 the *St. Magnus* (III) made a voyage from Kirkwall Bay to Lerwick with a contingent of Royal Air Force units, returning on the following day. She departed again on 1st June 1940 and the evidence suggests that she went to Scapa Flow, berthing alongside at Lyness, where embarkation (presumably naval personnel) took place that afternoon. She sailed on 3rd June arriving at Rosyth the following afternoon where her 'passengers' disembarked. She left Rosyth on 8th June probably for Scapa/Kirkwall where 43 officers and 305 other ranks of army personnel had embarked. The *St. Magnus* (III) sailed around 13.00 on 16th June, arriving at Aberdeen at 05.00 the following morning where the troops disembarked.

War losses were the *St. Fergus*, following a collision, and the *St. Catherine* (II) by bombing, both in 1940. The *St. Clement* (I) was lost by bombing in 1941. The *St. Sunniva* (II) foundered without trace off Newfoundland in January 1943 with the loss of 64 crew.

SERVICES FOLLOWING THE WAR

At the end of the war in Europe on 7th May and Japan on 14th August 1945, the North Company services were still essentially on a wartime footing, although the *St. Clair* (II) had been handed back to the company at Aberdeen on 19th June for refitting. There were still four allocated ships in the fleet (the *Blyth* and three General Steam Navigation Co. vessels) serving traditional ports. In addition a further two vessels had been allocated on 16th December 1944 as military transport. These were the *Nova* (Bergen Steamship Company) normally operating Aberdeen-Faroe (until September 1945) and the *Lochnagar* (Aberdeen Steam Navigation Company Ltd.) normally operating Aberdeen-Lerwick (until February 1946). Owned vessels on their regular services were the *St. Magnus* (III), St. *Rognvald* (II), *Rora Head*, *Dunleary*, *St. Ola* (I) and the *Earl of Zetland* (II).

The *St. Ninian* (I) and the *Earl of Zetland* remained as naval and military ferries on the Pentland Firth.

There was a general derequisition of all allocated vessels as from 2nd March 1946 once voyages were completed and the last of the 'outside' fleet departed on 26th March. However, with a severely depleted working fleet, the *Edina* was taken on commercial charter (March to June 1946), as was the *Naviedale* (April to June 1946). On the release of the *Earl of Zetland* from military duties, she returned to the North Isles route (December 1945 to March 1946), but was then transferred initially to the Aberdeen-Kirkwall service which had reverted to a twice-weekly passenger service before finally returning to her 'own' route. Her predecessor, the old 'Earl', was reallocated to the Pentland Firth for general assisting duties from December 1945 to early March 1946, followed by a final stint on the North Isles service until June 1946 when she returned to Aberdeen to lay up. The *Earl of Zetland* (II) was sold in November of that year and left Aberdeen on 5th December 1946 for a new life in the Mediterranean.

Above: The 1894-built **Amelia** *at Leith in the early fifties. (Ferry Publications Library)*

Right: The **St. Ninian** *(II) entered commercial service in 1950. Some 21 years later she was sold for further service. (Ferry Publications Library)*

For the period June 1945 to June 1946 there was an interim phase during which the Aberdeen-Kirkwall and Aberdeen-Lerwick services were provided on a twice-weekly basis. The Kirkwall route was provided by the *St. Rognvald* (II) or the *Earl of Zetland* (March to May) leaving Aberdeen on Tuesdays and Fridays and Kirkwall on Mondays and Wednesdays, while Lerwick was served by the *St. Magnus* (III) or *St. Rognvald* (II) (April to May), leaving Aberdeen on Mondays and Thursdays and Lerwick on Tuesdays and Saturdays. After a full year refitting and converting, which included conversion to oil burning, for her peace-time role, the *St. Clair* (II) took up the twice-weekly Lerwick service on 17th June 1946 and thereafter the 'direct' route but did not include a Leith call.

The indirect service resumed in July 1945 though there was one major difference. The main sailing was now one at the beginning of the week, normally Monday from Leith, while the secondary sailing left Leith on the Thursday. Initially the main sailing was operated by the *Blyth* or the *Aire* (September to November) but calls were not made at Aberdeen in either direction. This service terminated again in mid-December but resumed with the *St. Magnus* (III) in June 1946 on the traditional pattern of calling at Aberdeen both northbound and southbound. The most pressing problem for the company was the purchase of new tonnage and on 26th September 1946 the new *St. Clement* (II) made her maiden voyage from Aberdeen to Kirkwall. She replaced the *Dunleary* which had been sold the previous month to

Greek buyers. Like her earlier namesake she was a cargo ship but included some features not provided for on earlier vessels. While her predecessor had been provided with a saloon for the statutory twelve passengers, the new ship was fitted with 2-berth cabins for this number and the Master had the novelty of both a day room and a bedroom. One of the main duties envisaged for the *St. Clement* (II) was the carriage of livestock and she incorporated a ramped walkway from the upper (shelter) deck, accessible from the starboard side down to the main deck, so that livestock did not require to be lifted by crane off and on. There was also a portable walkway from the main deck down to the lower hold and during the major livestock movements this was regularly left in place. The *St. Clement* (II) fell into a fairly regular pattern during her early years of livestock sailings (September-November), secondary indirect service (November-May) and North Isles (March-April). At other times she effectively acted to clear backlogs or for supplementary sailings. The secondary indirect service had recommenced in September 1945 and notionally was operated fortnightly by the chartered *Edina*, but the service lapsed during March-May 1946. Like the main service, no Aberdeen calls were made in either direction. It reverted to something approaching its pre-war appearance from June 1946 when the *St. Rognvald* was allocated to the Thursday sailing from Leith. The main difference now was that the service terminated at Kirkwall all year round.

*Above:The **St. Ola** (II) at Stromness. She maintained the Pentland Firth crossing between 1951 and 1974. (Ferry Publications Library)*

NEW TONNAGE

The west-side service, effectively the Stromness boat with fortnightly calls at St. Margaret's Hope, was covered by the *Rora Head* although the *St. Clement* (II) was employed for periods during late summer and autumn, the *Naviedale* on charter was also used. The *St. Ninian* (I) was finally derequisitioned at Aberdeen in December 1946 and lay there unused for about two years before going to the breakers in 1948 at 53 years of age. Perhaps the most unusual feature of these immediate post-war years was that the *St. Rognvald* was used to relieve the Pentland Firth and the North Isles services during April/May 1947. Perhaps surprisingly it was not until 1950 before a main line vessel was built, though obviously the years of austerity and inflation in the immediate post-war period may have been the reason. The new vessel was the *St. Ninian* (II) and was innovatory in that she was the first twin-screw vessel in the fleet, indeed the only one until the car

ferries appeared 26 years later. She also introduced a rather different profile with only one hold forward and two aft. At 2,200 tons there was more scope in distributing the accommodation even though it was all concentrated in the mid-ships area. First Class cabins, mainly 2-berth with some 4-berth, were spread over four decks and, for the first time, the decks were identified A (prom deck), B (shelter deck), C (main or upper deck) and D (lower deck). Second Class cabins (4-berth and 6-berth) were situated on C and D decks. The Second Class dining room and the lounge/bar were located at the fore end of the accommodation block on B deck and the First Class dining saloon, seating 60, was located directly above. This was rather a high location for such a public room and during mealtimes caused continual difficulties in service in adverse weather conditions. As in the earlier *St. Clair* (II), there was an enclosed observation shelter surrounding the saloon on three sides and in the first year it had to

*The **St. Clair** (II) on trials during 1937. She was converted to oil burning in 1946 and renamed the **St. Magnus** (IV) in 1960. (Ferry Publications Library)*

serve as an overflow dining saloon during the peak season. It could seat a further 40 (later increased to 50) and meal service was only possible in that there were two communicating doors between the dining saloon and the observation area. There were very few cabins on A deck and the after end of this section was divided to form separate lounge and bar areas. The crew were located aft, the first time this had been done, although stewards were mainly on C deck (port side).

On the introduction into service of the *St. Ninian* (II) in June 1950 she was allocated to the main indirect route, displacing the *St. Magnus* (III) to the secondary sailings which now, as in pre-war years, was extended to Lerwick during the June-September period. The *St. Rognvald* operated the Stromness service that summer. The year of 1950 was the only post-war year that the company operated four main line vessels, still one less than in 1939. The *St. Rognvald* finished service in October 1950 and after

being laid up for a few months was sold to breakers. The *St. Ninian* (II) was thus effectively a replacement ship for the *St. Rognvald*.

The other improvement to services that summer was the re-establishment of the Caithness route and the *Rora Head*, being effectively surplus, was available to cover this route. One change was that Wick was the only Caithness route call until the end of October when Kirkwall was also included. From November the Caithness and Stromness services were generally operated jointly apart from the summer period.

In 1951 the final ship in the post-war reconstruction programme was built. This was the *St. Ola* (II) to replace her elderly 59-year-old namesake. She commenced service at the end of May 1951, her predecessor going to the breakers. In appearance she was an enlarged *Earl of Zetland* but had no well deck forward. With twin lifeboats on each side, she was easily distinguishable from the 'Earl'. Internally

Above: The **St. Magnus** *(IV) arriving at Leith in March 1966. (Ferry Publications Library)*

Right: The **St. Clair** *(III) dressed overall arriving at Lerwick on her maiden voyage. (Ferry Publications Library)*

the shelter deck had a large, rather spartan deck shelter on the fore end, while the after end was given over to a large well-furnished lounge/bar. The dining saloon was below this on the main deck and six 2-berth passenger cabins were located on the starboard side. There were also two rest rooms on the lower deck, male and female, furnished with settees and a comfortable area where passengers could lie down on a bad day on the Firth. The *St. Ola* (II) was also an innovatory vessel in that she was the first Single Class ship (cargo vessels excluded) in the fleet.

At the end of the war in 1945 the fleet consisted of ten vessels, including the two time-expired veterans (the *Earl of Zetland* (II) and *St. Ninian* (I)) with an average age of 37 years, four of the fleet being in excess of 50! At the end of this reconstruction programme six years later, the eight-strong fleet now averaged 15 years, although this still included the 57-year-old veteran *Amelia*.

THE TRADITIONAL PERIOD 1951-1974

This quarter century can perhaps be defined as a period of stability with no major changes, although the 'Steam Navigation' became the North of Scotland, Orkney & Shetland Shipping Co. Ltd. in 1953. Only three ships joined the fleet, one being second-hand, but four departed. It can be divided into two separate periods. From 1951 to 1966 services still largely followed the traditional pattern and with considerable resources devoted to expanding the all-inclusive cruise and hotel holiday concept. The period from 1967 to 1974 was one of contraction, other than on the freight side, when the main line fleet diminished to only one vessel and all services from Leith ceased.

In 1900 the company had built the St. Magnus

Hotel in Hillswick, Shetland, a four-month seasonal establishment which until 1939 had formed an essential seven-day stop-over link in the 12-day holiday packages from Leith/Aberdeen employing the services of the west-side steamer. The 1939 cost was £12 (Leith), £11.50 (Aberdeen). This particular 12-day holiday resumed in 1946 but as there was no longer a Hillswick vessel the 'cruise' part was in the care of the *St. Magnus* (III) or *St. Ninian* (II) from 1950 and passengers were taken by coach from Lerwick to Hillswick. In 1947 the Standing Stones Hotel at Stenness, Orkney was purchased, which was open all the year round and tourists could now select either hotel or have a week at both.

As the post-war austerity conditions diminished the company commenced 'signing up' various other local hotels acting as booking agents on their behalf. Three hotels in Shetland joined the scheme in 1955 and were all serviced by the *St. Magnus* (III) with her considerable passenger capacity. One hotel was on the island of Unst and this required 'cruisers' to transfer to the *Earl of Zetland* (II) to reach their destination. In 1956 the *St. Clair* (II) was brought into the range of holidays offered and five hotels participated that year. In 1957 an additional hotel was offered and it remained at five or six until 1965, although there were seven in 1959. In addition the two principal North Company hotels at Hillswick and Stenness continued to be served by the *St. Ninian* (II). Apart from all these inclusive cruise/hotel holidays, it was always possible to undertake the round trip on some of the ships as a pure cruise. These were certainly available from 1902 on selected

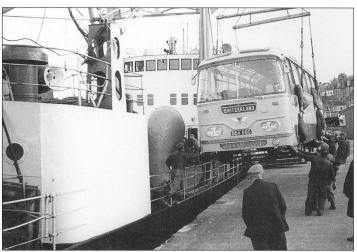

Above: Before the advent of ro-ro vessels coaches had to be crane-loaded onto the vessels. This picture shows a coach being loaded onto the St. Rognvald (III) at Stromness in 1966. (Ferry Publications Library)

machines and, most importantly, the access for the cattle ramp which linked the shelter deck with the 'tween deck. Unlike the *St. Clement* (II), this cattle ramp could be rigged at either side of the ship to suit loading requirements, though it was almost permanently rigged on the starboard side. Another innovatory feature was a heavy lift derrick for 15 tons, the other five derricks being for 3 or 5 tons.

Both holds were fitted for livestock carriage and there was a portable ramp installed to load livestock into Number 2 hold, something which previously had only been fitted to the *St. Ninian* (II). The *St. Rognvald* (III) largely took over the duties of the *St. Clement* (II) and normally spent September/October on livestock traffic which saw her visiting Baltasound and Fetlar occasionally, as well as the main ports. During the winter she operated what was effectively

vessels and from 1950 were available on any of the passenger vessels and from 1955 included the cargo vessels (12 passengers) as well. One trip which was very popular was the mini-cruise, though this descriptive title was not used until 1972. Their origin can be traced back as far as 1898, although at that time they could only be arranged on a stage-by-stage basis and involving a main line vessel to Lerwick before transferring to the *Earl of Zetland* and returning similarly. From 1946 the mini-cruise was offered as an all-inclusive *St. Clair/Earl of Zetland* package and the basic concept exists to this day, albeit without the North Isles extension, employing the ro-ro ferries.

The company had been considering a new ship for some time, one which can perhaps be considered an 'intermediate' vessel, as her design was for only 50 passengers and she was envisaged as the Caithness steamer with her other main role being to relieve the main line vessels when they were off on annual refit. Perhaps the additional trade anticipated during the construction of the various nuclear installations at Dounreay, only a few miles west of Scrabster, had influenced this decision. Whatever the reason, the design was significantly altered after the order was placed. What appeared in 1955 was a large cargo vessel with cabins for 12 passengers, eight of which were single-berth, an innovation in the fleet. This was the *St. Rognvald* (III) and she introduced a completely new profile to the fleet with all aft superstructure. There was a large deckhouse amidships extending from side to side and this incorporated store rooms, the cargo refrigerating

The St. Clement (II) of 1946 at Scrabster. (Ferry Publications Library)

*The **St. Clair** (III) leaving Lerwick for Aberdeen in the evening sun. (Ferry Publications Library)*

*The **St.Ola** (II) berthed at Stromness following her morning arrival from mainland Scotland. (Bruce Peter collection)*

the secondary indirect service vessel, while the *St. Magnus* (III) was relieving on other routes. In the spring and summer she normally operated a freight service to Kirkwall, St. Margaret's Hope (fortnightly) and Stromness.

On the introduction of the St. *Rognvald* (III), the *Amelia* was withdrawn and scrapped and the *Rora Head* generally covered Cooper's freight service, sometimes loading in Leith at both Cooper's and the North Company berth. In 1956 the Caithness service was withdrawn due to high operating expenses and the *Rora Head* was sold to Lerwick owners. The *St. Clement* (II) had also taken over some of the Cooper's sailings and it was around this time that Cooper's shed and office at Leith was relinquished and all the traffic concentrated at the Victoria Dock complex. It was also around 1954 that the company started the practice of calling at non-standard Orkney ports during March/April. About 4/5 sailings would be made calling at Stronsay, Sanday and Westray, and occasionally Longhope, normally combined with Caithness and Stromness sailings. The *Amelia* was employed in 1954, the *Rora Head* in 1956 and the *St. Clement* thereafter for about a decade. Cargoes were invariably manufactured manures and feeding stuffs for livestock. By 1956 with the introduction of the *St. Rognvald* (III), the sale of the 61-year-old *Amelia* and the 35-year-old *Rora Head*, the fleet was reduced to seven ships, with the average 13 years. This included the elderly *St. Magnus* (III) which had been built in 1924. However, when the *St. Rognvald* (III) joined the fleet the opportunity was taken to modernise the *St. Magnus* (III) and she was withdrawn from service for three months (February-May 1956) to be converted into an oil-burning vessel. The Second Class and crew's accommodation was remodelled from dormitory style to cabins. The First Class accommodation was less affected but the 18-berth ladies' cabin was converted to two 4-berth and one 6-berth cabins, and additional showers and toilet facilities were also installed. Like many of the earlier ships, some of the deck areas were convertible, i.e. First Class cabins in summer, livestock accommodation in winter! On the *St. Magnus* (III) this latterly consisted of a block of twelve 2-berth cabins (converted from dormitory style earlier) and these were altered to provide four 4-berth and eight 2-berth cabins. (These cabins were forever known to the crew as the 'cattle stalls' with the resultant entertainment of the occupants when they found out.) A further two 2-berth cabins were built on the shelter deck amidships. These alterations still provided berths for 224 First Class passengers, only ten less than the originally built arrangement.

ENTER THE THIRD ST CLAIR

Another main line vessel joined the fleet in 1960 in the form of the *St. Clair* (III) and although significantly larger (3,302 tons) than the *St. Ninian*

Another view of the St.Ola (II) inward bound to Scrabster late in her career with Dunnet Head in the background. (Lawrence Macduff)

(II), perhaps surprisingly, was a reversion to single screw. She had a more 'built-up' profile than anything previously, and reverted to the two holds forward and one aft. The four deck infrastructure allowed cabins to be located higher with all First Class completely above the waterline. The dining saloon was located aft of the engine casing, reverting to the shelter deck, thus at the same level as her namesake. First Class cabins were distributed over four decks and consisted of four 4-berth and eighty-two 2-berth. As with the *St. Ninian* (II), the Second Class was located in the forward section of the midships superstructure. Her namesake had been renamed the *St. Clair II* some time earlier and the introduction of the new *St. Clair* (III) resulted in the *St. Magnus* (III) being sold for scrap. The *St. Clair II* was then renamed *St. Magnus* (IV). The new *St. Clair* (III) took up the direct Aberdeen-Lerwick route, while the *St. Magnus* (IV) transferred to the secondary indirect route.

In 1961 the fortnightly call to St. Margaret's Hope had been reduced to a call every third week and 3rd May 1966 marked the withdrawal of calling there. The entire fleet was affected by the lengthy seamen's strike between mid-May and the beginning of July although the *St. Rognvald* (III) had been allowed to make a few trips with emergency supplies. The first ship to resume sailing was the *Earl of Zetland* (II) (Lerwick-Kirkwall-Aberdeen), bringing down the 'North' company seafarers to crew the fleet which was laid up in Aberdeen and Leith.

Towards the end of 1966 it was announced that the *St. Magnus* (IV) was to be withdrawn and would be replaced by a cargo/livestock vessel. The *St. Magnus* (IV) was renamed the *St. Magnus II* in October and she is unusual in having operated under six different names under the one ownership: *St. Clair*, HMS *Baldur*, *St. Clair*, *St. Clair II*, *St. Magnus* and *St. Magnus II*. Her replacement was the *City of Dublin* (Palgrave/Murphy) which was overhauled and converted for North Company service at Ardrossan over six months and entered service on 30th March 1967 from Leith on the secondary indirect service. She had been renamed the *St. Magnus* (V) a

*The **St. Clement** (II) is seen here at Lerwick during her layover at the port on 8th October 1972. (Lawrence Macduff)*

*The **St. Ola** (II) arriving at Scrabster on 5th August 1974. The **St. Clement** (II) is at berth while assisting the **St.Ola** on the route with car traffic during the summer peak period. (Lawrence Macduff)*

*The **St. Ninian** (II) leaves Leith for Aberdeen on one of her final sailings. (Lawrence Macduff)*

*The **St. Clair** (III) makes an impressive view inward-bound to Lerwick on 4th June 1976. She is pictured here with a black hull, pale blue funnel and flying the P&O house flag. (Lawrence Macduff)*

*The **St. Magnus** (V) at Aberdeen on 31st May 1976 with a pale blue funnel. (Lawrence Macduff).*

*The **St. Clair** (III) arrives in the early morning sunshine on 4th May 1975 at the port of Aberdeen. (Lawrence Macduff)*

fortnight earlier and at a distance was almost indistinguishable from the *St. Rognvald* (III). The main line fleet was now down to only two vessels. This also resulted in the contraction of the cruise/hotel programme, only three hotels being signed up for the 1967 and 1968 seasons, although the *St. Ninian* (II) continued additionally to serve Hillswick and Stenness hotels.

An unusual situation occurred in February 1970 when the *St. Clair* (III) was chartered to relieve the Liverpool-Belfast service for about two weeks while the *Ulster Queen* and the *Ulster Prince* were on survey. This arrangement was repeated in 1971 but covered four weeks and was facilitated by the fact that both companies were part of the Coast Lines Group which had taken over the North Company in 1961.

Early in September 1970 the company had discussed their plans with the local island authorities for the restructuring of the fleet and services. This envisaged three ro-ro vessels, one each for the Pentland Firth, Lerwick and Kirkwall routes, the last one being a 12-passenger vessel, but none would be in service before 1975. In addition Leith would be closed down and the *St. Ninian* (II) would be withdrawn. Stromness (apart from the Pentland Firth sailings) would also fall victim, all of these changes targeted for early 1971.

The final scheduled Stromness call was made on 24th February 1971 by the *St. Clement* (II), but it was stated that calls would be made if inducements were favourable. There were a few infrequent isolated calls thereafter. The *St. Magnus* (V) made the final sailing from Leith on 9th March 1971. The *St. Ninian* (II) which was relieving the *St. Clair* (III) made her last sailing when she arrived in Aberdeen on 28th February and was subsequently sold to Canadian interests, leaving Aberdeen on 26th April 1971 with basically a North Company crew on the delivery voyage. The Lerwick service continued to operate from Matthew's Quay, but Orkney freight services were transferred to Jamieson's Quay, which was the Coast Lines complex and the basic pattern became: the *St. Rognvald* ex Aberdeen (Mondays), Kirkwall (Tuesdays), Lerwick (Wednesdays), Aberdeen (arr Thursdays). The *St. Clement* ex Aberdeen (Tuesdays), Kirkwall (Wednesdays/Thursdays), Aberdeen (arr Fridays). The *St. Magnus* ex Aberdeen (Tuesdays), Kirkwall (weekend), Aberdeen (arr Tuesdays).

While this appeared to be poor utilisation of vessels, it eliminated expensive weekend discharging of cargo and the three vessels were basically required in that the *St. Clement* (II) normally spent ten weeks in the summer assisting with car traffic on the Pentland Firth and many additional sailings would be required during the autumn livestock season while allowances had to be made for the annual refits of all six vessels. During 1971 only the *St. Clair* (III) was advertised in the summer season brochure,

but 1972 saw a reversion to the indirect service being promoted (either the *St. Rognvald* (III) or the *St. Clement* (II), depending on whether early or late summer) and from May 1972 this sailing included a Kirkwall call southbound, arriving Aberdeen on Friday. A further contraction in the operations was the sale of the St. Magnus Hotel, Hillswick around May 1972, the Stenness Hotel having been sold as far back as 1953 although still included in the holiday packages up to 1970.

In October 1972 yards in both the UK and Europe had been requested to tender for a new ferry for the Aberdeen-Lerwick service. Meanwhile, the contract was given to Hall Russell, Aberdeen for a new Pentland Firth ferry on 12th December for delivery during spring 1974.

In perhaps the worst mishap since the war, the *St. Rognvald* (III) ran aground on Thieves Holm (Kirkwall Bay) on 4th May 1973 and was re-floated two weeks later. As the *St. Ola* (II) was off on refit at the time, the *Clarity* was chartered for about two weeks until her return. The *St. Rognvald* (III) returned to service on 25th June.

P&O TAKEOVER SERVICES

The Aberdeen-Lerwick ro-ro ferry order was eventually given to Hall Russell's at Aberdeen in July 1973 for delivery in May 1975; but the shipyard subsequently withdrew from the contract citing pressure of other work and it was back to square one. Coast Lines who had been taken over by the P&O Group in February 1971 looked at other vessels in their fleet that might fit the role instead of a newbuild. Two vessels were considered in late 1974, the *Lion* (Burns & Laird) and the *Norwave* (North Sea Ferries).

The new Pentland Firth vessel, the first ro-ro ferry in the fleet, the *St. Ola* (III) was launched at Aberdeen on 24th January 1974 with delivery planned for mid-June. It emerged that the first choice of name had been the *St. Olaf*, perpetuating the name of the first North Company vessel to operate on the route, but that name was unavailable. In preparation for the arrival of the new ferry the existing vessel on the route had been renamed the *St. Ola II*. The new *St. Ola* was delayed and made her visit to the Firth of Forth in mid-September for dry docking and speed trials, and then carried out final trials in Aberdeen Bay on 29th October 1974, later sailing overnight to Stromness. By arrangement, she met up with the *St. Ola II* off Houton (near Stromness) at 09.00 the next morning, subsequently berthing at the linkspan. An official reception was held on board for local dignitaries on the arrival day and the *St. Ola* (III) was open to the public on 31st October. On 1st November local schoolchildren were granted a special holiday and 420 visited the new ship. However, the delays at the shipyard paled into insignificance compared with the delays at Scrabster where the terminal was nowhere near ready. The *St. Ola* (III) lay unused for three months at Stromness before entering service.

Another part of the operations which had been seeing significant changes was on the North Isles of Shetland. In the summer of 1970 Zetland County Council received approval for their inter-island car ferry service which would attract a 75% Government Grant. At that stage this required four vessels and ten purpose-built terminals, although a fifth vessel (spare) was later added to the initial concept. The *Earl of Zetland* (II) was 31 years old and replacement by another conventional vessel was not a realistic option. The first of Zetland County Council's ferries, the *Fivla*, entered service on 21st May 1973 between Toft (mainland) and Ulsta (Yell), and after a transitional period the *Earl of Zetland* (II) progressively dropped her various calling ports in the North Isles as each new ferry was introduced. Calls at Mid Yell (Normally Thursdays) and Cullivoe, Yell (Fridays only) were discontinued after 1st August 1973, while final calls at Uyeasound, Unst (Mondays/Tuesdays overnight and Wednesdays, Fridays/Saturdays) and Baltasound, Unst (Fridays/Saturdays overnight) were made on 14th and 15th December respectively. The latter two ports were actually 'closed' by the *St. Ola II* which was on relief duties at the time. The overnight stopovers which had been part of the North Isles' history since 1877 terminated after 97 years, not quite making their century. From 17th December 1973 a new pattern of services commenced:

Mondays only Lerwick 8.00 – Whalsay, Skerries, Fetlar, Whalsay, Lerwick (arr c. 17.00).

Wednesdays only Lerwick 09.00 – Whalsay-Lerwick (arr c. 12.00).

Fridays only Lerwick 10.00 – Whalsay, Fetlar, Whalsay, Lerwick (arr c. 17.00).

Meanwhile on 22nd November the final Fetlar call was made.

In June 1974 the *Ortolan* of GSN (General Steam Navigation another division of Coast Lines/P&O) appeared on an inter-group charter and assisted the *St. Clair* (III) with freight trips. However, the first practical signs of the North Company's involvement with North Sea oil was imminent when she made a number of trips to Flotta (which eventually became the Occidental Oil Company oil terminal) and also called at Lyness. The *Ortolan* appears to have been employed intermittently until mid-December.

THE NEW GENERATION OF FERRIES

On 26th January 1975 the new *St. Ola* (III) made a circumnavigation of Hoy for crew familiarisation purposes to test all machinery systems. On the 28th she made a VIPs crossing to Scrabster and on the following day she made her maiden voyage from Stromness to Scrabster. At long last ro-ro had come to fruition, some eleven years after its introduction

in MacBrayne territory in the Western Isles. With her better speed, some schedule adjustments were made and were ex Stromness 08.45, ex Scrabster 12.00 (formerly 08.30/13.00). Internally the passenger accommodation was confined to the shelter (or upper deck) with a large observation saloon at the fore and a cafeteria/bar at the after end which was divided down the centre line on an open-plan layout. An entrance foyer and purser's office was amidships. Vehicles had the use of the entire main deck with two wing decks above accessed by lifts and frequently used for livestock.

The *St. Ola II* departed for Aberdeen on 29th January 1975 and after a few days was sold for use as a seismic survey vessel. Less than a month later the *Earl of Zetland* made her final voyage on 21st February. As a mark of the close relationship between the ship and the community, the crew on the *Earl of Zetland* held a private dinner party on board that evening and a few days later were the guests of the Provost at a reception in Lerwick Town Hall. A week later she left Lerwick for Aberdeen, played out by the town band, and was sold for further work as a seismic research vessel. Latterly she had been serving Whalsay and Skerries only and Zetland County Council took over the Skerries route from the end of February 1975. While all five of the Zetland County Council ferries had now been delivered, there were no terminals ready at Symbister (Whalsay) or Laxo (mainland) to allow the Whalsay service to operate. Instead, the *Grima* from the quintet was chartered by the North Company and provided a Symbister-Lerwick service until January 1976 when the Zetland County Council ferry service commenced. She was island-based and the schedule was ex Symbister 09.00 Tuesdays only and 07.30/13.00 Fridays only and ex Lerwick 14.00 Tuesdays only and 10.00/16.30 Fridays only.

Meanwhile during March 1975 the *Lion* was put out to tender for conversion to become the Lerwick ferry, but mounting losses on P&O's long routes (Lisbon, Tangier and San Sebastian) forced a rethink and in October it was announced that the former *SF Panther* (Southern Ferries of the P&O Group) would be employed instead! She had operated on the Southampton-San Sebastian route until its closure in 1973, and then had been chartered out to Da-No Linje for service in Norway and renamed the *Terje Vigen*. With what was effectively a five-ship fleet, which only included one ro-ro vessel, a relief vessel had to be chartered from outside. The *Clansman* (Caledonian MacBrayne) relieved the *St. Ola* during the first half of November that year and in fact fulfilled this role every year until 1982/83.

While the *St. Clair* and the three cargo ships continued as before, the most significant change during that first year of ro-ro was that the Pentland Firth sailings were increased during the summer. The old *St. Ola* had operated extra summer

*The **Earl of Zetland** (II) laying off Houbie, Isle of Fetlar during livestock movements on 15th October 1973. The 'flitboat' is astern of her. (Lawrence Macduff)*

*The **St. Clair** (III) laid up at Grangemouth at the end of her career. (Bruce Peter collection)*

*Above: The **St. Clement** (II) at Kirkwall unloading cargo prior to her departure to Lerwick. (Lawrence Macduff)*

*Right: The newly delivered **St. Ola** (III) on berthing trials at Scrabster prior to entry into service. (Ferry Publications Library)*

crossings for many years, but these were invariably only as required and traffic patterns generally confined these to the Friday to Monday period while Sunday sailings had become part of the advertised schedule from 1959 (July/August only) onwards. From the beginning of June the *St. Ola* (III) made an extra 15.00 Wednesdays only crossing from Stromness while on Thursdays five single crossings, commencing at 08.45 from Scrabster, were provided until the end of August. This was mainly to provide a day excursion on Thursdays from the Caithness side but on a number of occasions the Wednesday evening service was employed for charter cruises along the coast or through Scapa Flow and this arrangement continued for a number of years.

At the beginning of October 1975 the North Company title disappeared, the company initially trading as P&O Ferries (Orkney & Shetland Services) and the *St. Ola* (III) reappeared from refit in November with P&O pale blue funnels, the first of the visual alterations.

During 1974 preliminary site work had commenced at Aberdeen and Lerwick terminals though the construction phase did not commence until 1976 at Aberdeen and effectively became an extension of the then current Kirkwall freight berths. In the same month all vessels commenced using the new Lerwick facilities at Holmsgarth except for the *St. Clair* (III) which continued to use the 'mail' berth at Victoria Pier. The Matthew's Quay complex at Aberdeen was finally vacated at the end of October with the *St. Clair* transferring to a temporary berth at Regent's Quay.

In 1975 indications that North Sea oil was to be a major force, particularly in the northern North Sea, resulted in the freight-only ro-ro vessel the *Helga*

being purchased by P&O for management by the North Company. She was renamed the *Rof Beaver* (Rof signifying 'roll-on freighter'), the 'Beaver' being in accord with P&O's then stated policy of using the Burns' fleet animal names for all their ferries. She was Leith-based and with no North Company presence there by then, agents were appointed to look after her. She carried no passengers and the accommodation block was sited right aft. Loading was via the stern ramp and there was a large hold beneath the vehicle deck which could be conventionally crane-loaded. She was overhauled in Marseilles and made her delivery voyage to Immingham in May, loading for Sullom Voe. During that first year she visited Peterhead, Belfast, Stromness, Sandwick (Shetland) and Lerwick, as well as her more frequent visits to Flotta and Sullom Voe. She even got as far as Rotterdam on one occasion!

The *Ortolan* was again also frequently employed on charter, obviously on oil-related work, and she visited Leith, Inverkeithing, Dundee, Peterhead, Flotta, Kirkwall, Sandwick and Sullom Voe. Sister vessel the *Oriole* also made a few appearances apparently on traditional North Company routes from Aberdeen to Kirkwall and Lerwick.

In the islands there was continuous criticism of the 'blue' funnels which became more vociferous at the thought that their cherished 'Saint' names could disappear to be replaced with 'animal' names, but this criticism was allayed when an announcement was made that the *SF Panther* would be renamed the *St. Clair* (IV). The blue funnels remained but the 'Beaver' was to be the only 'animal' to enter the fleet list.

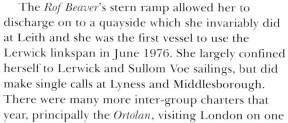

*Above: The newly built **St. Ola** (III) fitting out at Hull Russells Shipyard, Aberdeen in 1974 prior to entry into service. (Lawrence Macduff)*

The *Rof Beaver*'s stern ramp allowed her to discharge on to a quayside which she invariably did at Leith and she was the first vessel to use the Lerwick linkspan in June 1976. She largely confined herself to Lerwick and Sullom Voe sailings, but did make single calls at Lyness and Middlesborough. There were many more inter-group charters that year, principally the *Ortolan*, visiting London on one

occasion with the *Petrel* and the *Dorset Coast* also making appearances. One non-P&O vessel to be chartered was the *Rosemarkie* which briefly appeared, apparently on traditional freight work. At the beginning of December 1967, the *St. Clement*, the smallest of the freight ships, was sold to the Greeks and renamed the *Aghios Georgios*.

With the entry into service of the *St. Clair* (IV) on 4th April 1977, Shetland now had full ro-ro services to the outside world. A new lower fares structure from the islands (southbound) was introduced at this

*The **St. Clair** (IV) leaves Aberdeen for Shetland in April 1979, with her black livery and blue funnel prior to receiving the new P&O livery. (Lawrence Macduff)*

The **St. Clair** (IV) leaving Aberdeen on 12th April 1982 with the P&O house flag on her funnel. (Ferry Publications Library)

time. The *St. Clair* (III) was re-registered as the *St Clair II* to release the name for the new *St Clair* (IV), she then continued to make some freight sailings, including two indirect route sailings, relieving the *St. Rognvald* (III) and making rare calls at Kirkwall. She finished early in June, being sold on as the *Al Khairat* to the Meat Foodstuff Company of Kuwait.

The *St. Ola* (III) had a breakdown at the start of 1977, running on reduced power at first and missing some sailings if the weather was poor. The *St. Magnus* (V) was called in to take some cars south from Kirkwall to Aberdeen (New Year holiday traffic) while the *St. Rognvald* (III) helped out with an extra crossing of the Pentland Firth. In May 1977 the *St. Magnus* (V) was sold on to Sun Star Lines of Limassol, Cyprus as the *Mitera Eirina*. The *Ortolan* and the *Petrel* had again helped out on the freight side in September 1976, with the *Petrel* again in June 1977. The *Lairdsfox* and the *Dorset Coast* also appeared in June 1977 and from July to September 1978. In September 1977 the *Ortolan* finished with the P&O Group.

Livestock sailings by chartered tonnage on an annual seasonal basis commenced with the *Angus Express* on 17th September 1977. This situation was a result of the introduction of ro-ro operations and the demise of the *St. Magnus* (V) and the *St. Clement* (II). This arrangement continued until 2007 for periods of one to three months annually. These livestock sailings have gradually ceased making local calls with both island groups, concentrating on Lerwick (Shetland) and Kirkwall (Orkney). Aberdeen is the principal mainland port, but Invergordon and Peterhead have been used occasionally.

The *Bussard*, a Danish ship, was chartered for

three to four weeks for services from Aberdeen to Kirkwall, sometimes extending the service to Lerwick. The ro-ro freighter *Dorset* appeared on charter in February 1978 to relieve on the freight side on the Pentland Firth, after which P&O (Orkney & Shetland Services) decided to purchase her and to send her to Belfast for refit. She took up services in the North with the name *St. Magnus* (VI) on the indirect service, substituting Stromness for Kirkwall, immediately causing consternation with the authorities in Kirkwall who saw a need for a linkspan to retain links with Aberdeen and the South! The *Dorset* was built as the *Donautal* in 1970.

The *St. Magnus* (VI) started a Scandinavian service to Hanstholm in Denmark and Kristiansand in Norway. A regular pattern emerged which fitted in with her other duties while the *St. Rognvald* (III) was sold to Naviera Winton S/A Panama as the *Winston*.

A chartered Norwegian vessel, the *Nornan Fjord*, brought in animal foodstuffs to the islands over a ten-day period while the following year she reappeared as the *Sea Fisher* (Fishers of Barrow) to relieve the *St. Magnus* (VI). The *Condor* also appeared for a month to help out.

Fares were increased in March 1980 and brought a change to the rebate system, an increase on the passage subsidy and also a subsidy for accompanied cars from the islands.

A second linkspan, the Eurolink, in Aberdeen Harbour was used by one of the charter ships and was to be used by company ships on occasions over the years.

The Highlands and Islands Development Board (HIDB) was set up to promote development in the

Highland area and produced a report suggesting that Scrabster should be the port for Shetland. However, this was not acceptable to the Shetlanders who campaigned to keep the Aberdeen connection.

When the *St. Magnus* (VI) was overhauled in 1982 some Orkney-bound freight was sent by road to Scrabster from Aberdeen. This set a trend for the future and road improvements north of Inverness reduced the overall journey times to the Caithness port.

The *Smyril*, a car and passenger ro-ro ferry of Strandfaraskip Landsin (Faroese Government Shipping Department), was used to relieve the *St. Magnus* (VI), which in turn relieved the *St. Clair* (IV) and also the *St. Ola* (III). The *St. Magnus* (VI) made a trip for the *Rof Beaver* on 1st March 1982 incorporating a return visit to Leith.

In May 1982 the *St. Clair* (IV) was used for a fund-raising event for the Lerwick Lifeboat and this became an annual event, as did the cruise around Bressay and the bird sanctuary at Noss. The *Earl of Zetland* had previously made this cruise on similar charters during the fifties!

In autumn 1982 the *Smyril* relieved the *St. Clair* (IV), followed by the *St. Ola* (III). The *Smyril* had to return to the Faroes before the *St. Ola*'s (III) refit was complete and the *St. Magnus* took over for the short time until the *St. Ola* (III) was able to return to her route. A fire aboard the *St. Ola* (III) delayed her return and the *St. Magnus* (VI) was then assisted by the *Rof Beaver* and the *Orcadia* when she was available. In late November the *Clansman* of

*The **Rof Beaver** arriving at Leith in May 1985. (Lawrence Macduff)*

Caledonian MacBrayne was called in to cover the route. In January the *Clansman* had to return to service on the West Coast and the interim arrangements were resumed, i.e. the *St. Magnus*, the *Rof Beaver* and the *Orcadia* working the route between them until the *St. Ola* (III) resumed service on 7th February 1983. During this time when the *Orcadia* was on the Pentland Firth she sailed from Kirkwall to Scrabster but on at least two occasions she called at Wick. Meanwhile, Brittany Ferries' *Penn-ar-Bed* relieved the *St. Clair* (IV) for two weeks in February 1983.

On 9th May there was an unusual sailing to Gothenburg by the *St. Clair* (IV) for the final of the European Cup Winners Football Cup (Aberdeen versus Real Madrid) which Aberdeen won. A mini-

*The **St. Ola** (III) passes the Old Man of Hoy inbound to Stromness on 17th May 1991. (Lawrence Macduff)*

*The **St. Clair** (IV) and **St. Magnus** (VI) at Berths 3 and 4 Holmsgarth, Lerwick unloading following their arrival overnight from mainland Scotland. (Lawrence Macduff).*

cruise to Bergen took place in September 1983.

The *St. Ola's* (III) next relief was carried out in 1984 because of her fire the previous certificate had been issued in the spring of 1983, and from then on her overhaul was in the January-February period. The *St. Magnus* (VI) was given a passenger certificate for 50 passengers on the Pentland Firth crossing so she was used now regularly to relieve the *St. Ola* (III).

The *Smyril* was again used for relief duties in 1984

*Brittany Ferries' **Penn-ar-Bed** relieved for the St. Clair in February 1983. (Ferry Publications Library)*

for two weeks at which time the *St. Clair* (IV) was refitted with extra cabins. During May the ship offered a mini-cruise to Harlingen in Holland.

The *Norrona*, owned by Smyril Lines (a Faroese privatised company), had replaced the *Smyril* on the link between Faroe, Shetland and Norway in June 1983 and in 1985 they advertised through links to Britain using P&O (Orkney and Shetland Services) as their UK agents.

The Highlands and Islands Development Board and Orkney Council assisted some local shareholders to set up a new company, Viking Island Ferries, to operate a service linking Orkney with Shetland. They chose Kirkwall, Westray and Scalloway as their ports. The *Devonian* (ex *Scillonian II*) was the ship chosen. She arrived at Westray from Torquay on 17th November 1985 and visiting Kirkwall the following day and was renamed the *Syllingar*. The ship made her maiden voyage on 15th December but the service suffered from breakdowns and weather problems and by May 1986 the company was in receivership.

DAILY SAILINGS TO SHETLAND

P&O announced at this time that they would acquire a second passenger ship/ferry to operate the Aberdeen, Stromness, Lerwick route and additional direct sailings between Aberdeen and Lerwick.

The *nf Panther*, formerly of P&O Normandy

*The **St. Magnus** (VI) at Lerwick on her early evening arrival at the port in May 1988. (Lawrence Macduff).*

*The **St. Sunniva** (III) makes a fine sight as she passes Erskine in the River Clyde on 14th May 1988, following her appearance at the Garden Festival at Glasgow. (Colin J. Smith)*

*Above: The **St. Ola** (III) pictured at Govan, Glasgow following her overhaul and repainting with the P&O Ferries livery. (Lawrence Macduff)*

*Right: The **St. Sunniva** (III) and **St. Ola** (III) at Stromness in March 1989 following the introduction of the darker-blue livery of P&O. (Lawrence Macduff)*

Ferries' Dover-Boulogne route, was purchased by the company. Built as the *Djursland* for Jydsk Faergesfart of Denmark in 1972, the contract to refit her was awarded to Hall Russell's Aberdeen shipyard. The ship was refitted as an overnight ferry with cabins forward on main and upper passenger decks with restaurant, shop, TV room and bar from aft of mid-ships on the main deck. A self-service restaurant-cum-cinema aft doubled up with reclining seats as the overnight lounge on the upper deck, with more cabins on the port side aft.

The proposed pattern of services was: Mondays to Friday evening departures northbound and southbound on Sundays to Thursdays with an additional Saturday midday sailing northbound via Orkney. The Friday sailing southbound was to leave Lerwick at midday via Orkney. The *St. Clair* (IV) would take the Monday, Wednesday and Friday northbound sailings while the second ship would take the Tuesday, Thursday and Saturday northbound sailings. Sailings on a daily basis to Shetland for passengers had returned.

In 1986 the *Orcadia* was chartered to P&O to operate a weekly inter-island service from Kirkwall to Scalloway and on occasions diverted to Lerwick.

The *St. Magnus* (VI) continued on the *Rof Beaver*'s roster until the *nf Panther* was ready for service. Plans were made to have more mini-cruises for the spring and autumn when the new ship took up the routes but the *St. Clair* (IV) eventually undertook most of them. Mrs Olivia Ford renamed the *nf Panther* the *St. Sunniva* (III) on 27th March 1987. The bridge windows were damaged on the maiden voyage and electrical problems resulted in the ship having to return to Aberdeen but the special party of invited guests were given a later opportunity to sail on the *St. Sunniva* (III). A decision to use stronger

glass in all forward windows was made after this voyage!

In 1987 the brochure had a two-page feature on the 150th anniversary of P&O with various events taking place, e.g. the opening of the Bod of Gremista (birthplace of Arthur Anderson, founder of P&O Company), two visits to Leith on consecutive weekends, and an Orkney week promotion was held in Aberdeen.

The *St. Magnus* (VI) now regularly used the Eurolink. She was chartered to the Ministry of Defence in November 1987 when she sailed to Loch Ryan in south-west Scotland. The *St. Sunniva* (III) became the relief vessel for the fleet from 1988 onwards.

Plans to visit the Glasgow Garden Festival in summer 1988 were announced in the autumn of 1987. The *St. Sunniva*'s (III) Glasgow visit was incorporated with a southbound direct sailing to Aberdeen from Lerwick, returning to Stromness, with passengers who boarded at Aberdeen, before cruising through the Western Isles to Glasgow. Sadly due to industrial action the passengers had to be flown north after an extended visit to the Glasgow Garden Festival, where the ship was used as a floating exhibition centre for isles businesses.

In January 1989 the company changed the title of their North services once again when P&O Scottish Ferries was adopted. P&O took over their own dock labour staff on the demise of the National Dock

The **St. Sunniva** (III) at Stromness in the morning sunshine during her first season with P&O Scottish Ferries, prior to her departure for Shetland in the early afternoon. (Lawrence Macduff)

Labour Scheme.

In 1989 the *St. Magnus*'s (VI) freight sailings to and from Leith were altered to Grangemouth for six/eight weeks while the dock gates in Leith were being repaired.

The *St. Clair* (IV) made a mini-cruise to Maloy in Norway in spring 1989. At this time she was involved with further safety exercises involving Lifeboat, Coastguard and Military personnel as guinea pigs to test evacuation procedures. The *St. Clair* (IV), and later the *St. Ola*, came under close scrutiny as the costs of new safety measures, said to be in the order of £335,000 for the passenger fleet, were implemented following the *Herald of Free Enterprise* ferry disaster. It was suggested by company officials that the *Norrona* should be bought to replace the *St. Clair* (IV).

The *St. Sunniva* (III) added mid-week northbound calls each Tuesday at Stromness during the peak season, leaving Aberdeen at midday and Lerwick at midday on Wednesdays. This was linked with a call of about an hour and a half in each direction at Stromness from 1989.

A freight service to Hanstholm (Denmark) was again suggested in 1988 and an additional freight ship was required for this service, so a charter of the *Marino Torre* from Italian owners took place in 1989. She had 50% more freight capacity than the *St. Magnus* (VI) so she was eventually bought in as her successor on the indirect service. She was renamed

the *St. Rognvald* (IV) which had been built as the *Rhonetal* in 1970 at Lubeck, Germany.

The *St. Magnus* (VI) was relieved by the *Juniper* of Limassol in July 1989 before leaving for a charter on the Southampton to Cherbourg service and being offered for sale. The *Smyril* was chartered briefly to operate the new Scandinavian link and also operated on the Stromness to Lerwick service while the *St. Magnus* was away. A second-hand replacement for the *St. Clair* was now planned and £15 million set aside for this purpose.

The *St. Clair* (IV) took part in the Forth Bridge Centenary celebrations opened officially by HRH Prince Edward who switched on the floodlighting.

Mr Graeme Dunlop was brought in to manage this northern outpost for one year while Eric Turner became Chairman of Lloyd's Register of Shipping (Scotland).

During the overhaul period in 1992 the *St.*

The **St. Clair** (IV) arrives at Aberdeen from Lerwick. (Lawrence Macduff)

*A morning scene in May 1991 at Lerwick with the **St. Rognvald** (IV) and **St. Sunniva** (III). (Lawrence Macduff)*

*The **St. Ola** (IV) leaves Stromness for Scrabster in August 1993. (Lawrence Macduff)*

The **Tregastel** of Brittany Ferries was purchased by P&O for the Shetland Isles service in 1991. The vessel was converted and entered service as the **St. Clair** (V) the following year. (Miles Cowsill)

The **St. Clair** (V) leaves Lerwick in the evening sunshine for Aberdeen. (Colin J. Smith)

*The **St. Clair** (V) makes an impressive view off the coast of Shetland outward-bound from Lerwick. (Miles Cowsill)*

*The **St. Clair** (V) arrives at Aberdeen on 19th March 1993 in the morning sunshine from Lerwick. (Lawrence Macduff)*

*The **St. Sunniva** (III) swings off the berth at Stromness to allow the **St. Ola** (IV) to use the berth. (Miles Cowsill)*

Rognvald was damaged in heavy weather, requiring to be towed to Aberdeen when the *Smyril* was chartered for a week to cover. During this time she combined the rosters of both the *St. Sunniva* (III) and the *St. Rognvald* (IV). At this time it was announced that the *Smyril* would operate to Aberdeen on its Faroese service in lieu of Scrabster.

In 1991 the link had been maintained by the *Teistin*, another Faroese Government ship.

THE SECOND GENERATION OF FERRIES

The *Tregastel* of Brittany Ferries was bought in 1991 to commence service in 1992. She was sent to the Lloyd Werft yard at Bremerhaven for conversion work to be done. The *St. Ola* (III) was to be replaced by the *Eckero* ex *Svea Scarlett* of Eckero Lines of Finland.

The Stromness berth was proving too short for both the *St. Sunniva* (III) and the *St. Rognvald* (IV) and so work was put in hand to extend it. While this was being done the *St. Sunniva* (III) served Kirkwall in lieu of Stromness on some sailings and the *St. Rognvald* made additional calls there in addition to her Monday calls. The *St. Ola* (III) spent more time at Scrabster, sometimes on 'light' sailings as well as others already timetabled.

In the summer of 1991 the Tall Ships Race was staged at Aberdeen and the *St. Sunniva* was used by VIPs reviewing the fleet cruise.

In 1992 the *Tregastel* joined the fleet as *St. Clair* (V). Built as the *Travemunde* in 1971 for Moltzau Line (predecessors of Gedser – Travemunde Ruten), with a gross tonnage of 4,231, she had four passenger decks and two car/vehicle decks and was the largest ship in the fleet. The passenger cabins were mainly on C and D decks; the bar, lounges, restaurant, children's play area, and ship's office on B deck, and the reclining seat lounge on A deck.

In preparation for her own replacement on the Pentland Firth service, the *St. Ola* (III) was given the

*The **St Ola** (IV) at Scrabster during her last month in service on the route prior to the arrival of NorthLink operations. (Willie Mackay)*

*Above: The **St. Rognvald** (IV) at her berth at Lerwick pending her evening departure to Aberdeen. (Miles Cowsill)*

*Right: A wintry scene with the **St. Ola** (IV) at Scrabster with the impressive Ward Hill behind her. (Willie Mackay)*

suffix 'II' before retiring to Leith on the sale list. The *St. Clair* (IV) was also given the suffix 'II' but on 26th February 1992 was sold to Malaysian interests. Before entering service the *St. Ola* (IV) visited Kirkwall on a 'show the flag' cruise. As visits had been made to Scapa Pier by previous incumbents of the name this was an unusual occurrence. Stromness and Scrabster visits and berthing trials then followed and the *St. Ola* (IV) entered service on Wednesday, 25th March 1992. The main deck had a television lounge forward, ship's office in the foyer, restaurant and shop, while the bar was on the upper deck. She was built by Jos L. Meyer at Papenburg in 1971 as the *Svea Scarlett*. The *St. Ola* (IV) had a gross tonnage of 4,833, a length of 86.3 metres (283 ft.) and a service speed of 15 knots. She was able to carry 500 passengers and up to 110 cars and/or 20 commercial vehicles. As the *Cecilia*, the old *St. Ola* (III) was chartered to Svenska Rederi A.B. for a Denmark to Sweden crossing but was eventually sold

to Greek owners.

The *St. Ola* (IV) made her first visit to Lerwick after the *St. Sunniva* (III) had an engine failure and was grounded at Stromness. She made her crossing on Saturday evening, arriving on Sunday morning and leaving an hour or so later, reaching Stromness in the late afternoon and taking up her Scrabster sailings in the evening. Her return sailing was cancelled on the occasions this happened.

When it was announced that the *Norröna*'s calls at Lerwick were to cease at the end of August 1992, pressure from the Local Authority, Tourist Board and others led to a decision to send the *St. Clair* (V) to Bergen in the high season of 1993. This used the Friday departure from Aberdeen at 18.00 to Lerwick, departing from Lerwick during late Saturday mornings for Bergen arriving at 22.00 local time with the return sailing to Lerwick and Aberdeen two hours later. This renewed a link with the past when the North Company had offered Norwegian sailings for 23 years until 1908. This service continued in June, July and August for the next three years with slight timetable adjustments.

The *St. Rognvald* (IV) was the relief vessel in most winters, releasing the *St. Sunniva* (III) in the January

*The **St. Sunniva** (III) swings off the berth at Stromness while relieving for the **St. Ola** (IV). (Willie Mackay)*

The **St. Clair** (V) prepares to sail from Lerwick during her last season in service with P&O Scottish Ferries. (Miles Cowsill)

The *St. Rognvald* (IV) was chartered at summer weekends to Ferrymasters for their Middlesborough to Gothenburg service during 1993 and in 1994 she was chartered to Color Line for their Tyne to Bergen route. She continued with her own single weekly round trip to the Northern Isles during these years.

A report at this time suggested that a complete fleet replacement would cost around £100 million. Napier University suggested that using aluminium-constructed catamarans, each costing £40 million, up to 800 passengers and 100 cars could be carried, thereby saving up to two-thirds of the journey time to Shetland.

In 1993 investigative reports for H.I.E. and Shetland Islands Council into more economic ways of providing ferry services to and from Aberdeen suggested that the Government provided and owned the ships, with P&O Scottish Ferries or others managing them.

to March period to relieve the *St. Ola* (IV) and the *St. Clair* (V) to have their own overhauls. The *St. Rognvald* (IV) was usually overhauled first for a week or so and the *St. Sunniva* (III) made her own regular sailings to clear backlogs in traffic which occur each year.

The **St. Ola** (IV) at Scrabster in her last months of operation. The building works for the new linkspan for NorthLink operations can be seen behind her. (Willie Mackay)

The Era of NorthLink

TENDERING FOR THE ROUTES

By 2002 the Northern Isles stood at the edge of the most significant changes to their shipping services since the arrival of P&O Scottish Ferries.

The introduction of new freight services to Orkney and Shetland by Orcargo, which ceased to trade in 1999, and Streamline Shipping, led to overcapacity reducing the viability of the existing lifeline services provided by P&O Scottish Ferries. As a result the existing Tariff Rebate Subsidy (TRS) scheme was replaced, with a block grant system from 1st May 1995, with the new system benefiting a single carrier on a competitive tender basis for car and passenger traffic only. TRS had been divided amongst all of the available operators. Only livestock sailings would continue to receive subsidy on the TRS basis until 2006, when TRS was deemed to be unlawful under EU State Aid Rules. In the summer of 1995, the Scottish Office invited companies to tender for the new contract to serve the Northern Isles but the west coast operator Caledonian MacBrayne was excluded from the tendering process. The General Election and change of Government in May 1997 led to delays in completing the tender process and on 24th July 1997, the new Secretary of State for Scotland, Donald Dewar MP confirmed that P&O Scottish Ferries had won the contract for a further five years in the face of competition from Sea Containers and Orkney Ferries. However, with the P&O vessels ageing, new Safety of Life at Sea (SoLAS) regulations being introduced (with which the ships may not comply) and Scottish devolution on the horizon, a new tendering process for the operation of the

services beyond 2002 would begin almost immediately. This time around, Caledonian MacBrayne could participate and expressions of interest were invited in summer 1998.

Meanwhile, on Saturday 28th November 1998, the *St. Ola* (IV) departed from Stromness on her morning crossing of the Pentland Firth. As she headed east through Scapa Flow on account of a heavy westerly swell, an unfamiliar ship with a much more modern profile emerged from the mist off Cava and slipped into the vacated pier at Stromness. The mystery visitor was the three-year-old Caledonian MacBrayne ferry *Isle of Lewis,* making a courtesy call to Orkney on her return from her annual overhaul on the Tyne. During her four-hour visit she was opened to the public and the modern facilities of the *Isle of Lewis* impressed Orcadian residents, councillors and business people alike. Caledonian MacBrayne had made their intentions clear – they intended to compete strongly for the privilege of serving the communities of Orkney and Shetland.

'CAL MAC AND FRIENDS'

On 17th December 1999, the Scottish Executive, answerable to the Scottish Parliament on transport matters, announced that four companies – P&O Scottish Ferries, Serco/Denholm, Sea Containers and Caledonian MacBrayne and its partners – would be invited to submit tenders by March 2000 to operate the new contract. As part of their respective tenders, the participating companies were obliged to make public their plans for the future services. The P&O tender was initially based on acquisition of second hand vessels for the Aberdeen routes and engine upgrading/replacement on the *St. Ola* (IV). The deadline was extended to the end of May 2000 during which time P&O revised their proposals to include new ships at a cost of around £100 million with the proposed vessels very similar to those which subsequently appeared with NorthLink. The company appeared confident of continuing their association with the Northern Isles. The Serco/Denholm bid was based on a single passenger vessel operating on a 24-hour basis. Such a service – daytime one-way and overnight the other – would have been unlikely to meet the main customer requirement for an end of day departure and overnight crossing. Additionally, the timetable was tight and allowed no flexibility for bad weather or other delays. Meanwhile Sea Containers withdrew from the bid process.

Caledonian MacBrayne anticipated growth on the

*The **Isle of Lewis** made a courtesy call to Stromness on 28th November 1998. (CalMac)*

*P&O Scottish Ferries **St. Clair** (V) makes a majestic departure from Aberdeen on 26th June 2002. (Colin J. Smith)*

*The **St. Sunniva** (III) leaves Aberdeen on her midday departure outward bound for Stromness and Lerwick. (Colin J. Smith)*

*Top: A courtesy visit to Stromness by the **Clansman** on 31st January 2000. (Willie Mackay)*

*Above: This view shows **St Sunniva** (III) leaving Stromness for the last time on 14th April 2002. (Andrew MacLeod)*

*Right: Old and new at Aberdeen as NorthLink's **Hjaltland** waits at Regent's Quay pending berthing trials, whilst the P&O ferry **St. Clair** (V) prepares to depart on 18th September 2002. (Colin J. Smith)*

routes, estimating around £8 million greater passenger revenue than P&O. They led a consortium which included the Royal Bank of Scotland, funders and owners of the new ships, the Isle of Wight ferry operator WightLink, National Express and the shipbuilders Ferguson of Port Glasgow and Devon-based Appledore Shipyard. In the event final consortium was an equal partnership between CalMac and Royal Bank of Scotland with WightLink and other partners having ended their interest prior to submission.

During a courtesy visit to Stromness by *Clansman* on 31st January 2000, Caledonian MacBrayne gave details of the three new vessels they would provide if successful. Two large 12,000 GRT, 24-knot ferries with capacity for 600 passengers would be built for the two Shetland routes with an 8,600-ton, 18+ knot, 600-passenger, 110-car ferry for the Pentland Firth crossing. The initial Expression of Interest was submitted on behalf of 'CalMac and Friends' then changed to 'CalMac NorthLink' and finally to 'NorthLink'. Further work was required on trading names for the new company, with Norlantic being one option. However, the name 'NorthLink' was

subsequently adopted and continues to the present day.

The role of Caledonian MacBrayne in Northern Isles ferry services stems from 5th October 2000, when Transport Minister Sarah Boyack MSP announced to the Scottish Parliament that the Caledonian MacBrayne partnership with Royal Bank of Scotland was the successful tender bid and that the new operation would begin in late 2002. For P&O Scottish Ferries it was the end of a long history serving Orkney and Shetland, but for Caledonian MacBrayne, it was a significant, if somewhat logical extension of their operations. NorthLink Orkney & Shetland Ferries was quickly established and with headquarters in Stromness, they set about ordering the promised car and passenger ferries, for introduction in October 2002. Although CalMac was a joint venture partner providing technical and ship management services, NorthLink was to be an otherwise autonomous business with its own staff, management and way of delivering services.

FAREWELL TO P&O

The last days of the P&O vessels were not trouble free. The *St. Clair* (V) made her final sailing on 30th September 2002, operating the final northbound P&O Scottish Ferries sailing from Aberdeen to Lerwick. She sailed to Leith the next day and was subsequently sold to Saudi Arabian owners to be based in Jeddah for Pilgrim traffic on the Red Sea, under the name of the *Barakat*. Her new sphere of

Above: The **Faye**, *formerly the* **St. Sunniva** (III) *is framed by the bow of the new* **Hamnavoe** *at Leith on 5th November 2002. (Colin J. Smith)*

operation was thus a far cry from the wild seas of Shetland. On 26th October, en route to the Netherlands for overhaul she ran short of fuel off Hook of Holland and was towed into port by two tugs. She was still registered under the Saudi Arabian flag in 2009.

The final few months of the *St. Sunniva* (III) were full of minor incidents – a food poisoning scare, engine failure, repeated turbo charger problems and a cracked sewage pipe – all of which led to delayed or cancelled sailings and dry docking for repairs. With the imminent arrival of NorthLink in October 2002 and the need for the pier at Stromness to be upgraded in advance of the new services, the *St. Sunniva* made her last call on 14th April 2002. Using Kirkwall for the remainder of her season, she paid off on 30th September 2002, operating the final 18.00 hrs departure from Lerwick to be replaced next day by the new arrivals. She sailed to Leith for lay-up and was sold to Al Thurya of Dubai for further trading as the *Faye*. She departed from Leith on 15th November 2002 entering service between Dubai and the Iraqi port of Um Qasr in January 2003. Two months later, the US-led invasion of Iraq consumed the country and the *Faye* was subsequently scrapped at Alang, India in early 2005.

The future for the *St. Ola* (IV) was more auspicious. On 30th September 2002, under the command of Captain Willie Mackay, and with 147 passengers on board, she made her final sailing from Stromness to Scrabster, prior to sailing to Leith and

onwards to Estonian ferry operators Saaremaa Shipping Company. Her departure from Orkney brought to an end 110 years of continuous service of the four ships to bear the name *St. Ola*. Departing from Leith on Wednesday 9th October 2002, she passed her successor *Hamnavoe* off the south coast of Sweden and joined her near sister *Regula*, on the Kuivastu – Virtsu route. She occasionally reappeared

The **Barakat** *(ex* **St. Clair** *(V)) laid up at Rotterdam following her sale to Saudi Arabian interests for Pilgrim traffic operations on the Red Sea. (Ferry Publications Library)*

The **Hrossey** fitting out on 24th April 2002, with **Hjaltland** in the background. (Andrew MacLeod)

in Northern Isles waters when en route to the Faroe Islands to undertake relief sailings for the ferry *Smyril*.

The final sailing of the *St. Rognvald* (IV) for P&O Scottish Ferries took place on 28th September 2002, following which she was sold to Gulf Offshore of Aberdeen and chartered by the newly established Norse Island Ferries, continuing to serve Shetland for a time. By this fortuitous set of circumstances, one of the old P&O order had slipped through the net, albeit temporarily.

THE NEW FLEET ARRIVES

The new NorthLink vessels for the services from Aberdeen were impressive. Both were built by Aker Finnyards of Rouma, Finland at a contract price of around £32 million each and were designed specifically to serve the direct and indirect routes from Aberdeen to Lerwick (Holmsgarth) via Kirkwall, where they would use a new terminal at Hatston, rather than Stromness. In effect, the Kirkwall call revived in its entirety, the former 'North Company' indirect route. Timetables for the

The **Hjaltland** at the fitting out berth, after float out from the building dock. The funnel of Tallink's **Romantika** is in the background. (Andrew MacLeod)

The **Hrossey**'s prefabricated bow section including clamshell bow doors was built in Poland. It is shown here being hoisted for welding onto the forward section of the ship. (Andrew MacLeod)

The **Hamnavoe** pictured in the building dock on 28th May 2002. (Andrew MacLeod)

An aerial view of all three Northlink vessels in their final stages of construction. (STX Europe)

*The **Hjaltland** undergoing painting works in the dry dock at Aker Finnyards, Rouma. (STX Europe)*

new, faster vessels would be markedly different from their predecessors, with later departure times from Aberdeen and earlier island arrivals. NorthLink would operate 7 days per week and offered 12-14 hour crossings even travelling via Orkney which now received calls on 4 days a week northbound and 3 days a week southbound, thus opening up major new inter-island opportunities as well as giving Orkney residents a new Kirkwall - Aberdeen service which has been heavily used from the outset.

There were to be no more 'saints'. The names chosen for all the three new ships and the fourth vessel – a somewhat elderly but reliable freight vessel

– were chosen in a competition by island residents and reflected the desire of NorthLink to be very much at the heart of the islands, rather than being perceived as a company based in distant Aberdeen. Reflecting the Norse heritage of the Northern Isles, the two larger ships were named *Hjaltland* and *Hrossey,* these being the Old Norse names for Shetland and Orkney respectively. To cement their roots in the island communities, the company transferred as many P&O staff as possible into their fleet on similar employment terms. On 1st October 2002, the brand new *Hjaltland* set out from Aberdeen, bound for Kirkwall and Lerwick, whilst

*The **Hjaltland** nearest with **Hrossey** double berthed alongside the fitting out quay on 24th April 2002. (Andrew MacLeod)*

*The **Hjaltland** in her final stages of construction. (Andrew MacLeod)*

HROSSEY & HJALTLAND
(AS BUILT BY AKER FINNYARDS)

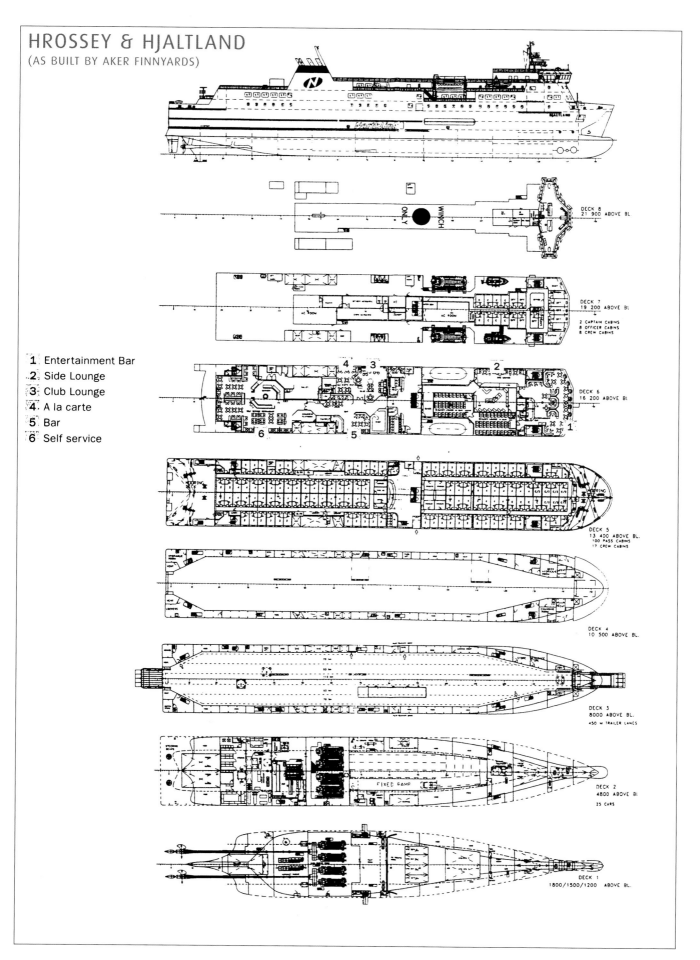

1 Entertainment Bar
2 Side Lounge
3 Club Lounge
4 A la carte
5 Bar
6 Self service

*The **Hjaltland** and **Hrossey** together at Leith for a VIP/Press reception on 23rd September 2002. (Andrew MacLeod)*

*The **Hjaltland** on sea trials off the coast of Finland. (STX Europe)*

the *Hrossey*, departed from Lerwick southbound heralding the dawn of a new era of ferry links between the islands and mainland Scotland.

HJALTLAND

Work started on the first vessel at Aker on 20th August 2001 when the project consultant John Horton symbolically stamped his initials onto a metal plate to be used in the steelwork of *Hjaltland* (yard number 438). Following Finnish tradition, the keel of *Hjaltland* was laid over 15th century 'good luck' *rheingulden* coins on 4th October 2001. The *Hjaltland* was floated out of her construction dock on 25th March 2002 and was delivered to her new owners on 12th August 2002. With the handover of the first ship, the new NorthLink Chief Executive, Bill Davidson, took up the post, having been involved in the project since its very earliest days. The *Hjaltland* departed from her builders on 16th August 2002 and sailed to Leith under the command of Captain David Wheeler who described her as "beyond expectations". Following further fitting out the *Hjaltland* was welcomed to the new Holmsgarth terminal at Lerwick for the first time on 12th September where she towered above the *St. Clair* and displayed the new NorthLink house flag, almost identical to that of the old 'North Company', except for a lighter shade of blue, thereby acknowledging the heritage of a bygone era. On 14th September she was named by Narene Fullarton who had suggested the ship's name, and was opened to the public at Victoria Pier where she met with favourable comment and was inspected by a significant proportion of the Shetland population. She departed for Aberdeen via Kirkwall where berthing trials took place at the existing P&O terminal at the Town Pier. The *Hjaltland* took up service on 1st October 2002, departing from Aberdeen on the first northbound sailing, complete with the 'Lerwick Up Helly Aa Jarl Squad' aboard to add to the celebrations.

HROSSEY

On 4th October 2001, Orkney Islands Council convener, Councillor Hugh Halcro-Johnston stamped his initials into steel destined for sister ship the *Hrossey* (yard number 439). The keel was laid on 1st December and the ship was floated out on 20th April 2002 then handed over to NorthLink on 7th September. The *Hrossey* left Rauma on 12th September and sailed to Leith, for a week of further fitting out with her master Captain Clive Austin describing her as "a wonderful, wonderful ship". She arrived in Kirkwall on the 24th September and, prior to opening to the public, was named by Kirsten Kelday, daughter of Alan Kelday who had suggested her name. On 1st October 2002, *Hrossey* undertook the first sailing southbound from Lerwick with thick fog delaying her arrival at Aberdeen for three hours.

*Another view of the **Hjaltland** and **Hrossey** together at Leith. (Andrew MacLeod)*

RAISING THE STANDARDS

Both *Hjaltland* and *Hrossey* are drive through ferries, 125 metres in length with a beam of 19.5 metres, gross tonnage of 12,000 and capacity for 600 passengers including 300 overnight berths. Both ships were designed by the Finnish marine design consultants Deltamarin, whose design stable includes an impressive pedigree of excellent ferries and cruise ships including *Disney Magic, Disney Wonder, Voyager of the Seas, Europa, Armorique, Ulysses, Viking XPRS* and vessels of the Superfast fleet from *Superfast I* to *Superfast XII*. Deltamarin also designed *Blue Star Ithaki* built in Korea in 2000 for Strintzis Lines whose parent company, Attica were sufficiently impressed with the NorthLink ships to make an unsuccessful offer to buy them in 2003.

Central to the NorthLink concept was the intention to offer passengers an altogether higher standard of service, with modern cruise-ferry style cabin accommodation, a choice of dining options, entertainment facilities, cinema, children's play area,

*On board the **Hrossey** at Kirkwall on 23rd September 2002 at the naming ceremony. From left to right: Rosie Wallace, Rebecca Parkin, Jim Wallace (Deputy First Minister), Hannah Barbour, Kirsten Kelday, Bill Davidson and NorthLink's Non Executive Director Lex Gold. (NorthLink)*

The **Hjaltland** leads her sister **Hrossey** as they pass beneath the Forth Bridge on 23rd September 2002. (Colin J. Smith)

The **Hjaltland** makes a fine sight in the evening sunshine as she passes the Forth Bridge on 23rd September 2002 carrying invited tourism industry guests on their familiarisation cruise (Colin J. Smith)

shopping and other on-board services including four disabled cabins. Interior design was undertaken by the Essex-based Lindy Austin Partnership and the new vessels' interior design reflected the close links between the ships and the two island communities which they would serve. Hence the *Hrossey* has an Orcadian theme and displays Kirkwall as her port of registry whilst the *Hjaltland* offers a Shetland theme and her port of registry is Lerwick.

The main reception foyer is located on Deck 5, from where two and four-berth ensuite cabins are located fore and aft on both sides of the vessel with the outside cabins boasting large windows. The reception area is floored with chequered polished granite incorporating a compass motif and is fitted with a large gently curved stone-topped reception desk behind which a model of the vessel is on display. A central stairwell leads up to Deck 6 where all other passenger facilities are located. The use of wood panelling effect, mirrors and stainless steel fittings gives both vessels a cruise ferry ambience with leather seating and carpets all of high quality. Each vessel has two bars, the Midships Bar and Filska Bar aboard *Hjaltland*, Midships Bar and Skyran Bar on *Hrossey* and in September 2004, well ahead of Scottish legislation, a no smoking policy was introduced, meaning that both vessels are now entirely smoke-free throughout their enclosed

spaces. Both the *Hrossey* and *Hjaltland* offer a cinema lounge incorporating recliner seats and airline style suspended LCD screens with headphones showing up to three films per evening. The Orcadian theme aboard the *Hrossey* is continued with the positioning of a contemporary 'leaping salmon' sculpture in the reception area adjacent to the central stairway, whilst aboard the *Hjaltland*, the position is occupied by a sculpture in stainless steel of a (left handed!) Viking warrior.

Both vessels boast impressive à la carte restaurants serving local products and cuisine from Orkney and Shetland, the Lönabrack aboard the *Hjaltland* and the Ladeberry aboard *Hrossey* together with excellent self service restaurants, the Braebrough aboard *Hrossey* and the Shoormal aboard *Hjaltland*. In March 2009, in response to demand, the number of covers in each of the à la carte restaurants was increased from 30 to 37.

Both vessels offer shops which stock the best of Shetland and Orkney crafts and produce, with a wide selection of jewellery, knitwear, wines and spirits, including Orcadian single malt whisky and Shetland gin, on offer.

External areas include a small gallery deck astern of the self service restaurant with stairways leading up to outside areas on the upper level above the crew accommodation block at bridge level. Crew

*The **Hjaltland** departing from Aberdeen on 18th March 2003. (Colin J. Smith)*

*Above: The Filska Bar on the **Hjaltland**. (STX Europe)*

*Right: The **Hjaltland** departs from Aberdeen whilst the paddle steamer **Waverley** rests at Atlantic Wharf during a break in her long trip from Great Yarmouth to the Firth of Clyde on 10th June 2003. (Colin J. Smith)*

accommodation, two rescue boats, a pair of lifeboats, fully enclosed bridge and officer's mess are situated on Deck 7 with a helipad located on the uppermost level, Deck 8. Navigational radar is carried on both ships' forward masts and both also possess stern radar for berthing.

Below decks main machinery consists of four medium speed 5,400 kW MAK 6M43 heavy fuel oil diesel engines, each pair driving a Kamewa 4.1 metre controllable pitch propeller through a gearbox and each vessel has two auxiliary heavy fuel oil diesel engine generator sets, as well as two shaft driven generators. Both ships are capable of a cruising speed of 24 knots, compared to the 16 knots of their predecessors, reducing the journey time on the direct route to Lerwick to 12 hours instead 14 hours by P&O. The *Hjaltland* and *Hrossey* can make the crossing in 8.5 hours if required as the vessel's four engines allow permutations ranging from very

economical through to flat out. When running on a single propeller, for example, the other can be fully feathered to minimise drag and can be 'parked' to align the blades with the A-frame thereby further reducing the drag effect.

To comply with SoLAS regulations, Deck 3, the vehicle deck, is over 1 metre above the waterline and offers 450 metres of 'truck-width' lane space whilst a lower garage on Deck 2 can hold 25 cars and is accessed via a fixed ramp. There are no cabins below the waterline. For the first time on Scottish-owned vessels, the bow doors were of the clamshell type, replacing the bow visor common on Caledonian MacBrayne vessels. Both vessels have a crew complement of 37.

*The Midships Bar on board the **Hjaltland**. (STX Europe)*

*Both the **Hjaltland** and her sister **Hrossey** offer the highest standards of navigational equipment. (STX Europe)*

*Wide staircases on both the **Hjaltland** and her sister **Hrossey** give ease of access all deck for passengers. (STX Europe)*

Prior to commencing service NorthLink organised a special event in Leith for the many people and firms who had been heavily involved in the creation of NorthLink, the design of the ships, the preparation of the winning bid to operate the lifeline services and the financing of the new ships. This 'corporate day' was then followed by a three-night trip to Orkney & Shetland for over 100 invited tourism industry guests from home and overseas. The trip, undertaken by the *Hjaltland*, launched NorthLink's drive to grow tourism to the Northern Isles through their 'NorthLink Cruise Tours' brand. On 23rd September, prior to departure from the Forth, the *Hjaltland* departed from Leith, having embarked her invited guests, and led the *Hrossey* on

a cruise upriver beneath the Forth Bridges to Rosyth, which had been adopted as Northlink's bad weather diversionary port.

The introduction of the new ships was accompanied by some of the worst weather ever experienced in the Northern Isles and North East Scotland but the vessels acquitted themselves well. Gale force winds on 21st October 2002 led to the closure of Aberdeen and the first diversion by the *Hrossey* to Rosyth. So severe was the weather that all NorthLink sailings were cancelled, resuming on 24th October 2002. On 3rd November 2002, the *Hrossey* encountered easterly Force 11 winds and seas so mountainous that she sought shelter to the west of Shetland, returning to Lerwick almost 24 hours after her departure with minor damage to her foredeck fittings. Meanwhile the *Hjaltland* on one crossing arrived in Lerwick after 40 hours at sea, having been forced to omit her Kirkwall call. However there were to be only three diversions in the next seven years. It was an unlucky start for the new service.

Initially, the two larger vessels experienced difficulties at Aberdeen on account of silting in the

*The car deck of the **Hjaltland** can accommodate up to 150 cars. (STX Europe)*

*The Shoormal self service restaurant on the **Hjaltland**. (STX Europe)*

HAMNAVOE

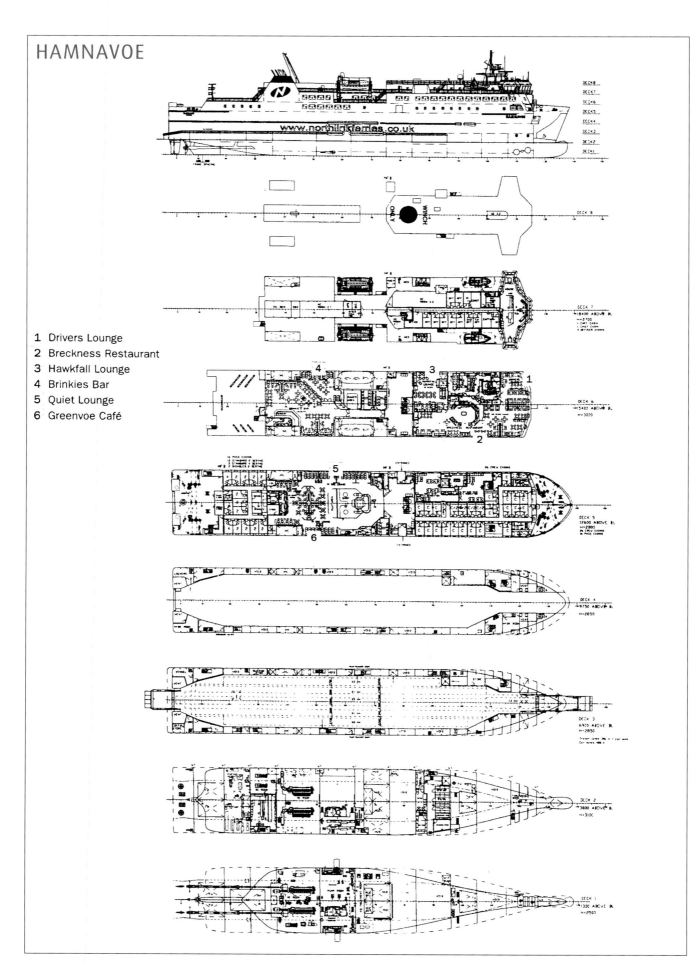

1 Drivers Lounge
2 Breckness Restaurant
3 Hawkfall Lounge
4 Brinkies Bar
5 Quiet Lounge
6 Greenvoe Café

*In her original condition the **Hrossey** makes a departure from Aberdeen for Kirkwall on 22nd April 2004. (Colin J. Smith)*

harbour channel, which was rectified by dredging in late 2002. Both the *Hjaltland* and *Hrossey* have regularly undertaken RNLI charters organised in Shetland and Aberdeen with the ships being made available at no cost whilst sponsors and suppliers donate services free of charge to ensure that 100% of ticket sales and bar and shop profits go to the RNLI with all the fuel costs being donated. In February 2009 both *Hrossey* and *Hjaltland* visited Fredericia in Denmark for overhauls which saw application of 'Intersleek 900' antifouling paint coating, a new low friction 'Teflon' style of paint, together with the construction of a forecastle deckhouse to prevent

recurrence of previous wave damage to the fo'c'sle doorway leading to the crew accommodation area.

In general, problems have been few and the ships have become accepted and admired by their many passengers over the years, whilst being immaculately maintained by their crews and officers who serve aboard with great pride.

HAMNAVOE

The £28 million *Hamnavoe* (yard number 440) was a smaller version of the new twins being 112 metres in length, having an 18.6 metre beam, with 306 lane metres of vehicle space giving capacity for 110 cars.

*Bill Davidson and Ron Montgomery (Royal Bank of Scotland) at the handover the **Hjaltland**. (NorthLink)*

The CalMac team at Aker Finnyards. From left to right: Norrie Brown, Phil Preston, Dr Harold Mills and Willie Paterson. (NorthLink)

*Above: The **Hebridean Isles** outward bound from Scrabster during her last few days on the route. (NorthLink)*

*Right: The **Hamnavoe** at Stromness following the completion of berthing trials for Pentland Firth service. (Andrew MacLeod)*

She has capacity for 600 passengers, including 32 overnight berths. A letter of intent to build the ship had been placed with Ferguson Shipbuilders of Port Glasgow in October 2000 but on 11th December 2000 Ferguson's notified NorthLink that they could not formalise the contract due to the tight 22-months deadline for completion. Within 18 hours a further letter of intent was placed with Aker Finnyards Shipyard in Rauma, with the contract signed for the third ship on 19th January 2001, the Aker yard being able to complete the smaller *Hamnavoe* thanks to a gap in their order book caused by lapsing of an option for SeaFrance. The keel of *Hamnavoe* was laid on 4th March 2002 and she was floated out on 5th June 2002, with confident predictions that, in spite of minor delays in construction, she would be ready for the 1st October commencement of the Pentland Firth service. In the event, although the *Hamnavoe* herself was ready, the new pier at Scrabster was incomplete. Aker had constructed the new vessel, from keel laying to handover, in less than 7 months.

*The **Hamnavoe** arriving at Scrabster for berthing trials. Work on the pier was at the time some seven months behind schedule. (Andrew MacLeod)*

The *Hamnavoe* arrived at Leith on Wednesday 9th October 2002 and had been given the Old Norse name for Stromness meaning 'Safe Haven'. En route she passed her predecessor *St. Ola* (IV) off the Swedish coast. She then visited Stromness where she was named on 19th October by her sponsor Linda Harcus, and was opened to the public for two days. Following this, she returned to Leith, sharing the Ocean terminal for a time with the former Royal Yacht Britannia and her predecessors *Barakat* (ex *St. Clair*) and *Faye* (ex *St. Sunniva*). She was laid up for seven months pending the completion of the new pier at Scrabster whilst the CalMac ferry *Hebridean Isles* provided the Pentland Firth service and experienced cancellations during the worst of the winter weather.

With more delays occurring on the completion of the new pier at Scrabster, an interface platform was built for the forthcoming season, during the calmer weather, to allow *Hamnavoe* to load from the old pier, which was not to be completed until September 2003 – a year late. It was not until 7th April 2003 that the *Hamnavoe* finally left Leith, undertaking berthing trials at Aberdeen, Lerwick, Hatston and Scrabster over the next few days. Following modifications to the old Scrabster pier to allow her to berth, she was open to the public at the Caithness port on 13th April 2003 and she undertook two Charity Cruises for the RNLI on Saturday 19th and Sunday 20th for the Stromness and Thurso branches respectively. She then spent two days 'shadowing' the *Hebridean Isles* on the Pentland Firth prior to taking up service on the 09.00 crossing on Monday 21st April 2003 but

*The **Hamnavoe** and **Hebridean Isles** pass each other in Hoy Sound, following the entry into service of the new purpose built vessel for the link on 19th April. (NorthLink)*

operating on a modified schedule until the new pier at Scrabster was completed.

Like her larger consorts *Hamnavoe* is fitted out to a cruise ship standard, the interiors having been designed by Lindy Austin Partnership who subsequently undertook the interior design for CalMac's Polish-built Islay ferry *Finlaggan*. On board facilities include the Breckness self service restaurant, the Greenvoe Café, the Hawkfall Lounge, Brinkie's Bar, which opens onto a large open deck area overlooking the stern, games room and a children's play area. *Hamnavoe* has twelve two and four-berth cabins for use mainly by passengers on the first departure of the day from Stromness. Being permanently associated with the shorter Pentland Firth crossing to Orkney, the *Hamnavoe* is registered in Kirkwall. The centrepiece in her reception area is a sculpture called 'The Mither o' the Sea', representing the benign force of the summer sea, one of the oldest elements of Orcadian folklore, whilst the writings of the celebrated Orcadian writer and lifelong Stromness resident, George Mackay Brown, author of the poem "Hamnavoe" are etched on glass throughout the ship. *Hamnavoe* is powered by two MAK 9M32 diesels, with an output of 4,340 kW driving two Kamewa propellers giving a service speed of 19 knots and has a crew of up to 39.

On 16th May 2004 *Hamnavoe* sailed to Bremerhaven, returning to service on 25th May where remedial work on fissures in the A-frame structures supporting the propeller shafts was carried out prior to the start of the main tourist season. Her replacement for a one-week period was the freighter *Hascosay* which carried all cars, freight and up to 12 passengers, with support from the John o' Groats ferry *Pentland Venture* to transport all other passengers. On 16th May 2006 the *Hamnavoe* struck the Outer Holm at the mouth of Stromness Harbour due to an electrical failure but was not damaged and in April 2008 during overhaul at Fredericia, she was modified to burn low sulphur fuel – a cheaper intermediate fuel oil instead of expensive gas oil.

To allow her to relieve the *Hamnavoe* the *Hjaltland* undertook berthing trials at Scrabster and Stromness on 14th April 2007 whilst en route to Birkenhead for overhaul and the addition of a new cabin block. Her first spell of service on the Pentland Firth took place between 13th and 29th April 2008, making her the largest vessel ever to serve on the Pentland Firth crossing, a task she has repeated in subsequent years.

THE NORTHLINK FREIGHTER

In addition to the three newbuilds, the company undertook to operate a fourth vessel for livestock and commercial vehicles only, acquiring the 6,136 ton vessel *Sea Clipper* and renaming her *Hascosay* after an uninhabited Shetland island lying between Yell and Fetlar. The *Hascosay* was built in 1971 at Kristiansand, Norway as the *Juno*, and was sold in 1979 to Finnfranline of France, being renamed the *Normandia* and was chartered to Finncarriers for service between Finland and France.

In 1982 she was chartered to Sucargo for service between France, Algeria and the Middle East. In 1986 she was sold to Mikkola of Finland, renamed the *Misidia* and chartered to Transfennica for services between Finland and Northern Europe. In 1990 she was sold to Kristiania Ejendom of Norway and was renamed the *Euro Nor*. In 1991 she was chartered to Commodore Ferries becoming the *Commodore Clipper*

*The **Hrossey** leaves Lerwick on her evening sailing to Orkney and Aberdeen. (Miles Cowsill)*

The **Hjaltland** arrives at Lerwick at 06.30 on her overnight sailing from Aberdeen. This view shows the additional accommodation which was added to the upper deck at the stern to provide further cabins. (Miles Cowsill)

An impressive view of the **Hamnavoe** approaching Rora Head, north bound from Scrabster. (NorthLink)

*Above: The chartered Norwegian freighter **Clare** departs from Aberdeen in the company of the harbour pilot launch on 21st April 2004. (Colin J. Smith)*

*Right: The **Hascosay** arrives at Lerwick inward-bound from Aberdeen. (Willie Mackay)*

serving the Channel Islands and in 1996 she was replaced by the *Commodore Goodwill* and sold to Goliat Shipping and was renamed the *Sea Clipper*.

In 1998, the vessel was chartered to the Estonian Shipping Company (Esco) for service between Germany and Estonia as the *Transbaltica*. In 2001 she was renamed the *Sea Clipper* and chartered to Fjord Line, prior to joining NorthLink early 2002. The *Hascosay* was an ice class vessel, able to carry over 36 trailers or, in livestock container mode, accommodate 5,500 lambs or 1,000 cattle on a daily basis as well as about 20 trailers at a maximum speed of over 17 knots. In preparation for her new role she underwent a major refit at the Remontowa Shipyard, Gdansk, Poland and entered service on 8th May 2002, not on Northern Isles services but on charter to Caledonian MacBrayne for freight runs between Ullapool and Stornoway. The *Hascosay* was the first

vessel to don the new livery of NorthLink Ferries and on 1st October 2002 she transferred to Aberdeen to take up the route for which she was intended, namely Northern Isles freight sailings.

During a period relieving for the *Hamnavoe* in May 2004, the *Hascosay* carried 12 passengers with her services supplemented by the John o' Groats passenger ferry *Pentland Venture* between the mainland and Burwick. By this time, her smart livery had given way to a more sombre dark blue hull, having failed to stand up to the rigours of winter on such an old ship.

HARBOUR INVESTMENTS

To handle the new ferries, major upgrading of terminal and berthing facilities at Aberdeen, Scrabster, Stromness, Kirkwall and Holmsgarth (Lerwick) was undertaken.

At Kirkwall, the construction of a completely new 161-metre Ro-Ro terminal at Hatston one mile north of Kirkwall facilitated the reintroduction of the seven times weekly indirect route, with vessels calling in each direction at Kirkwall on passage between Shetland and Aberdeen. In addition to the ferry terminal, Hatston offered a 225-metre deepwater berth for large cruise ships, rapidly becoming a central feature in the tourism industry in Orkney. The Hatston terminal opened on 21st October 2002. At Lerwick, the new Holmsgarth terminal, designed by the Aberdeen-based architects Arch Henderson,

*The **MN Toucan** was chartered for freight work during an extended absence of the **Hascosay** for rudder repairs in early 2007. (Willie Mackay)*

*Above:In her original NorthLink livery the freighter **Hascosay** is seen departing from Aberdeen on a sunny day on March 18th 2003 (Colin J. Smith)*

was opened on 1st April 2002. The terminal was also capable of accommodating the new 36,000 GRT Smyril Line vessel *Norröna*, introduced in 2003 to link Shetland with Iceland, Denmark and the Faroe Islands. Aberdeen also witnessed major reconstruction of the terminal areas in 2002/2003, with much of the life-expired P&O infrastructure at Aberdeen razed to make way for new marshalling areas and a new livestock shed. Aberdeen Harbour Board also provided a new award winning two storey passenger terminal designed by Arch Henderson, with covered boarding walkways and new check-in and luggage storage facilities.

At Stromness, the pier was strengthened and modified through addition of an upper level walkway and covered boarding bridge and replacement linkspan. In Caithness, construction of the new pier at Scrabster, named Queen Elizabeth Pier was delayed by around a year, being officially opened by HRH Prince Charles, the Duke of Rothesay on 6th August 2003 and the new passenger terminal at the pier became operational on 10th August 2004, almost two years after the start of NorthLink services.

FREIGHT AND LIVESTOCK

The movement of livestock and freight all year round is central to the economies of Orkney and Shetland. Prior to handover to NorthLink, the handling of livestock required to be modified to comply with the new livestock welfare regulations of the EU. NorthLink proposed to carry livestock using specially designed livestock 'cassettes'. Today, the company utilises a fleet of 12-metre and 6-metre trucks based on the MAFI lower running roll-trailers as used extensively in freight ro-ro services with double deck aluminium bodies. Forty-eight of these units were built by Stewart Trailers of Inverurie and in support of these trailers, new lairage facilities were provided at Lerwick, Hatston and Aberdeen.

As the peak livestock season straddled the change of operator from P&O to NorthLink, it was agreed that P&O would start and finish the 2002 livestock season, using the chartered *Buffalo Express* alongside the *St. Rognvald* during October 2002 even though their passenger services ended at the end of September.

*Livestock carriers, such as the **Buffalo Express** seen here leaving Aberdeen, were regular seasonal visitors to the Northern Isles prior to 2007 (Colin J. Smith)*

*The **Hamnavoe** loading cars at Stromness. (NorthLink)*

FREIGHT COMPETITION

In July 2002, the three main haulage companies in the Northern Isles - Northwards, JBT and Shetland Transport came together with Cenargo and Gulf Offshore North Sea to launch a new freight company, Norse Island Ferries. On 24th July 2002, the company announced it would link Aberdeen and Shetland from the end of August 2002 using the former Norse Merchant Ferries vessel, *Merchant Venture*, (1979) then laid up at Birkenhead and offering a service from Aberdeen and Lerwick six days a week with the *St Rognvald* following as their second ship in October 2002. For NorthLink, this represented the loss of about 90% of the freight on the existing route and as such was a major blow. Competition ensued, with the reliability of the new NorthLink ships proving increasingly popular for freight operators. The *Merchant Venture* proved troublesome, with NIF having to charter the *European Mariner* to cover for her extended absence due to mechanical problems. These problems led to the *Merchant Venture* being permanently withdrawn in February 2003. Meanwhile financial difficulties at Cenargo gradually impacted upon Norse Island Ferries and as a result, the company graciously bowed to the inevitable on 7th June 2003. For NorthLink, the demise of NIF saw freight demand increase sharply requiring additional capacity through the immediate charter of the erstwhile *St. Rognvald* to meet the additional demand. As a result NorthLink's costs rose dramatically in the wake of a period when freight traffic revenue had been significantly undercut, threatening the very survival of the company.

In November 2003 the *St. Rognvald* was sold to Middle Eastern interests and on to India for scrap in January 2004. She was replaced by the Danish vessel *Clare* on 5th December 2003. Built at Bremerhaven

*The **Hascosay** swinging off the berth at Lerwick inward-bound Kirkwall. (Willie Mackay)*

in 1972 as the *Wesertal*, she was renamed *Meyer Express* upon delivery, reverting to *Wesertal* in 1973. She subsequently carried the names *Vinzia E*, and *Dana Baltica*, when operating between Denmark and Lithuania for DFDS Baltic Line, and was subsequently operated by Smyril Line between Torshavn, Lerwick and Hanstholm between 2001 and late 2003, when she was chartered to NorthLink. On 30th July 2004, the *Clare* suffered an engine explosion, which necessitated her withdrawal for repairs, returning to service on 25th August during which time she was replaced by the *MN Colibri*, a ship employed in carrying components of the ESA Ariane rocket vehicle. A similar vessel, the *MN Toucan* was chartered for freight work during an extended absence of the *Hascosay* for rudder repairs in early 2007.

In support of the autumn livestock sailings, NorthLink continued to charter the livestock carriers

*A morning scene with the **Hrossey** inward-bound to Lerwick from Aberdeen. (NorthLink)*

Above: Pentland Ferries' **Pentalina B**, *formerly the Caledonian MacBrayne ferry* **Iona**, *is seen arriving at St. Margaret's Hope on 22nd May 2003. (Colin J. Smith)*

Right: The **Clare** *prepares for her morning sailing to Kirkwall. (Miles Cowsill)*

Buffalo Express or her near sister *Zebu Express*, for sailings from Aberdeen. These arrangements continued only until 2007 since when livestock sailings have been handled by NorthLink vessels using the new livestock containers which started to become available during 2008.

ORKNEY COMPETITOR

In 2001 a new company began sailings on the route between St. Margaret's Hope in Orkney and Gills Bay in Caithness, formerly the location of the terminal for the ill-fated Orkney Ferries short sea crossing venture in the 1980s. Pentland Ferries was the brainchild of Andrew Banks whose family had been involved in operating work boats at the Flotta oil terminal and who acquired the former Caledonian MacBrayne ferry *Iona* dating from 1970 and subsequently the 1979-built side loader *Claymore*,

An interesting collection of vessels at St Margaret's Hope. From left to right, the **Claymore**, **Pentalina B** *and the new* **Pentalina**. *(Willie Mackay)*

renaming the former the *Pentalina B*. The initial impact of Pentland Ferries was to attract around an estimated 30% of the 180,000 passengers conveyed by P&O on the Scrabster – Stromness route. However levels have since recovered with NorthLink's passenger numbers on the Stromness crossing steadily increasing by 55,000 between 2002 and 2005. Pentland Ferries now operate the *Pentalina*, an 18-knot RoPax catamaran with capacity for 30 cars and 250 passengers which was built in the Philippines in 2008.

Thanks to the new NorthLink vessels, the arrival of Pentland Ferries on the Pentland Firth and new competitors in the shape of Norse Island ferries, a total of eight large ferries were available to serve the Northern Isles from mainland Scotland for a time in 2002-2003. Islanders had never had it so good. But the good times could not, and did not, continue indefinitely.

'IT WASN'T BROKE. BUT IT IS NOW. AND HOW.'

So ran the editorial in the *Shetland Times* of 9th April 2004. On the previous day, the Transport Minister, Nicol Stephen MSP unexpectedly announced that as a result of huge trading losses at NorthLink, the tendering process would be repeated with a new contract to serve the Northern Isles coming into force in 2005, two years earlier than the planned date of September 2007. An additional £13.4 million had been made available to NorthLink between October 2002 and April 2004 to offset losses incurred as a result of unforeseen circumstances,

*The **Hjaltland, Clare** and **Hascosay** at Lerwick during a weekend lay-over. (Willie Mackay)*

including the need to charter the *St. Rognvald* and subsequently the *Clare*, which had adverse impacts on the NorthLink business plan.

The successful NorthLink bid had been prepared on the basis of historic traffic and market conditions data provided by P&O Scottish Ferries. But even before the arrival of NorthLink in October 2002, fundamental changes and unforeseen events had adversely affected the financial model on which the bid had been prepared and accepted by the Scottish Executive. These included delays due to Scrabster Harbour Trust being a year late in completion of facilities for the Pentland Firth service, the consequent tie up of the £28m *Hamnavoe* at Leith for six months, with the resultant revenue loss on the route, together with the need to charter the *Hebridean Isles* and the start-up of rival Pentland Ferries. The arrival and subsequent demise of Norse Island Ferries had an adverse effect on Northlink's fragile freight revenue, putting the company onto the financial back foot even before services began. Audit Scotland concluded that "NorthLink got into financial difficulties because competition reduced its income and some of its costs were higher than expected". The business NorthLink had planned to run was not the one they were actually running and by summer 2002 it was clear that refinancing was required.

The situation had been under discussion with the Scottish Executive since the summer of 2002 pending the outcome of a funding agreement that was acceptable to the European Union. NorthLink

continued to operate the services until a revised tender could be undertaken. Expressions of interest were invited in late April 2004 and the detailed tender was published on 27th May 2004. P&O announced withdrawal from the process on 30th June 2004 and on 19th July 2005, Transport Minister Tavish Scott MSP announced the tender shortlist and specifications, which included a reduced tariff for freight on the Aberdeen routes, improvements to the timetable and new provision for the carriage of livestock.

NORTHLINK 2

The NorthLink brand name, logo, and identity were offered for sale to bidders if they wished to use it. Three companies, V Ships UK Ltd, Irish Continental Ferries plc and Caledonian MacBrayne Ltd were invited to tender for the services, with

*The newly arrived **Pentalina** at Gills Bay. She was built in the Philippines in 2008. (Willie Mackay)*

*The weather conditions on the Pentland Firth can at times be very rough. This view shows the **Hamnavoe** outward-bound for Scrabster with the island of Hoy behind her in the setting sun. (Willie Mackay)*

*The small town of Stromness plays host to the cruise ship **Hanseatic**, while the **Hamnavoe** leaves for Scrabster. (Willie Mackay)*

THE ERA OF NORTHLINK

*A morning scene off Graemsay with the **Hamnavoe** inward-bound for Stromness. (NorthLink)*

operation and leasing of the NorthLink vessels transferring to the successful bidder. Although they had no involvement in the tendering process, the Royal Bank of Scotland would continue to own the three new ships, with a charter arrangement set up between the bank and the successful operator. In a memo to all staff on 19th July 2005, NorthLink CEO Bill Davidson made it clear that whilst his own companies' interest in the tender was at an end, a successful bid by Caledonian MacBrayne would effectively mean that NorthLink Ferries would continue as a wholly owned subsidiary of the West Coast operator, in the guise of what he termed "NorthLink 2". It was intended that services would transfer to the new operator on 1st April 2005 but the start date was revised to July 2006.

Only two companies submitted tenders, the Irish operator withdrawing from the process, and on 9th March 2006, Transport Minister Tavish Scott MSP, announced that Caledonian MacBrayne had been successful. Under the six-year contract, Orkney saw a 19% reduction in freight tariffs, while Shetland's reduced by 25%.

On 6th July 2006, control passed to the new operator, NorthLink Ferries Limited. This company was a wholly owned subsidiary of none other than the dormant David MacBrayne Ltd, (DML) which was reactivated to become the parent company of the operator of the Northern Isles contract. David MacBrayne Limited now owned NorthLink Ferries Limited and remained in the ownership of Scottish

Ministers, as did Caledonian MacBrayne Limited, which remained a separate operating company. The ships themselves remained the property of the Royal Bank of Scotland. To the travelling public, everything remained pretty much the same as before. Somewhere in heaven, old Mr. MacBrayne, master at last of all he surveyed, poured himself a celebratory dram.

The subsequent re-tendering of services and the takeover by parent company DML did not halt the growth in traffic generated by NorthLink. By 2007 it was necessary to increase cabin capacity on the larger ships by 20%, from 280 to 356 berths out of their total passenger complement of 600. To provide the additional berths on both vessels a new crew accommodation module was constructed on the deck above the cafeteria whilst existing crew cabins on the passenger cabin deck Deck 5 were refurbished for passenger use. The work was undertaken by Northwestern Shiprepairers at Birkenhead during annual survey and overhaul on *Hjaltland* during April and May 2007 and on *Hrossey* over a three-week period from 26th February 2007.

In summer 2009 NorthLink began consulting on possible changes to their schedules which would see the introduction of additional daytime sailings between Orkney and Shetland to free up overnight accommodation for passengers on Aberdeen – Lerwick sailings and with a reduction in winter time passenger capacity on the direct service. Responses to the proposals were mixed with the tourism

*The **Hamnavoe** undergoing her annual refit at Birkenhead. (Dick Clague)*

*Another view of the **Hamnavoe** under refit. Usually all NorthLink passenger vessels are withdrawn from service for around two weeks a year for overhaul. (Dick Clague)*

*The **Hascosay** was replaced in February 2010 by the **Hildasay** (ex **Shield**) on the freight services to Orkney and Shetland. (Willie Mackay)*

industry welcoming the proposed increases in summer passenger capacity whilst other sectors, mainly the aquaculture industry, were concerned about the effect on delivery times and winter capacity to Aberdeen and as a result the proposals were shelved.

The economic recession which began in late 2008 had an unexpectedly positive impact as NorthLink's passenger and freight carryings continued to increase throughout 2009. However with limitations on the capacity of the *Hascosay* NorthLink turned to the Irish Sea for a replacement. This was the 121 metre, 7,606 ton *Shield*, built in 1999 at Huelva in Spain for Esco. Following a refit at Birkenhead which included modifications to her stern ramp, the *Shield* was renamed *Hildasay* on 10th February by Shetland schoolgirl Sophie Wishart and took up service for NorthLink on 18th February 2010. The previous day the *Hascosay* made her last sailing from Lerwick to Aberdeen, having covered 432,000 miles for the company. On 13th March 2010 *Hascosay* departed from Kirkwall for the last time, her destination Beirut, where she would be refitted for another chapter in her long career as a livestock carrier sailing to Jordan from Brazil, Georgia and Romania.

NorthLink plan to replace the *Clare* by the end of 2010 with another freight vessel with similar capacity to the *Hildasay*

NORTHLINK FERRIES TODAY

Today NorthLink Ferries lies at the epicentre of island life. A trade route for agriculture, fisheries and businesses, and a transport link for residents, it is also a bringer of the essential tourism business which underpins so much of the island economies. The initial assertion that there was scope to generate growth in traffic to the Northern Isles has been borne out with around 150,000 passengers carried

per year between Aberdeen and Shetland, a 50% increase in traffic since P&O days and with a 250% increase in traffic between Aberdeen and Kirkwall. Yet EU bureaucracy means that NorthLink can never take for granted its position as the main ferry company serving Orkney and Shetland and preparing for the next round of tendering is an ongoing task.

NorthLink is a significant generator of employment in the islands and a strong supporter of community activities. The company employs around 70 shore-based staff, (about 50 full time) the majority in the islands, and employs 300 crew on its four vessels. Employees are drawn from the islands, from mainland Scotland and from further afield in the UK and overseas. The company's main office and call centre is in Stromness, located in the two-storey terminal building at Stromness Harbour. The company contracts out a range of services such as security, cabin cleaning and stevedoring and under the recently reorganised David MacBrayne Ltd it shares services with CalMac Ferries including crewing management, finance, and technical services.

*The **Hrossey** arrives on the Mersey for overhaul against a backdrop of the Liver Building and Liverpool waterfront. (Ian Collard)*

*The **Hrossey** leaves Lerwick on her evening sailing to Aberdeen with the island of Bressay behind her. (Miles Cowsill)*

NorthLink's Commercial Director Cynthia Spencer with Sophie Wishart and CEO Bill Davidson at the renaming of the **Hildasay***. (NorthLink)*

A full turnout for the renaming of the **Hildasay** *at Lerwick, including Jarl Squad. (NorthLink)*

To offer travellers a taste of the islands, NorthLink buys local goods and services as far as possible by applying its 'Buy Local Produce' policy through which it procures almost 40% of its food and beverage from island suppliers. Since 2002, NorthLink has supported events such as RNLI fundraising days, the NatWest Island Games, Tall Ships Race, Johnsmas Foy, Shetland Folk Festival, the European Fireball Championships, St. Magnus Festival, Shetland Classic Motor Show and Stromness Shopping Week. In addition, the £100k per year NorthLink Sponsorship Programme has supported individuals, local charities, community and sporting groups and athletes in Orkney and Shetland plus groups and individuals travelling from the Scottish mainland for events in the Northern Isles.

The ships themselves, flagships of the overall £100 million investment package, remain as superb as the day they first sailed, reflecting the great pride taken in them by their crews. They are still owned by the Royal Bank of Scotland on the basis of a 15-year ownership agreement over three tender periods meaning that any future operator would be able to use them, unless they opted to provide alternative vessels of their own.

At the outset of the service, there was some nervousness about the new era and indeed some the islanders suggested that the ships were too opulent for the Northern Isles whilst other commentators did not regard them as particularly beautiful. Inevitably there were yearnings for the old days of P&O and their predecessors. Over the years, however, the ships of NorthLink Ferries have won over the hearts and minds of islanders and visitors alike firmly securing their place as worthy successors to their predecessors and proud ambassadors for the people of Orkney and Shetland.

The **Hildasay** *alongside at Lerwick prior to taking up service. (NorthLink)*